TOUCHSTONES NOW

Michael & Peter Benton

Photo credits: **p.10** Striped Jug with Spring Flowers, 1992, Easton, Timothy (Contemporary Artist)/Private Collection/The Bridgeman Art Library **p.17** © 2006 Topfoto.co.uk **p.22** The Great Wave of Kanagawa, from the series '36 Views of Mt.Fuji' ('Fugaku sanjuokkei') pub. by Nishimura Eijudo, 1831 (colour woodblock print), Hokusai, Katsushika (1760–1849) /Christie's Images, Photo © Christie's Images/The Bridgeman Art Library **p.29** Mary Evans Picture Library **p.37** © Vintage Image/Alamy **p.44** Mother and Child (oil on canvas) by Previati, Gaetano (1852–1920) © Galleria Nazionale d'Arte Moderna, Rome, Italy/Alinari/The Bridgeman Art Library **p.55** The Old Ballad Singer, c.1780 (colour litho)/Guildhall Library, City of London/The Bridgeman Art Library **p.110** Mary Evans Picture Library **p.125** P.124–1950. pt43 The Tyger: plate 43 from 'Songs of Innocence and of Experience' (copy R) c.1802–08 (etching, ink and w/c), Blake, William (1757–1827)/ Fitzwilliam Museum, University of Cambridge, UK/The Bridgeman Art Library **p.134** Design 9 for 'Ode on the Death of a Favourite Cat' from 'The Poems of Thomas Gray', published 1797–98 (w/c with pen & ink on paper), Blake, William (1757–1827)/Yale Center for British Art, Paul Mellon Collection, USA/The Bridgeman Art Library **p.172** Landscape with the Fall of Icarus, c.1555 (oil on canvas), Brueghel, Pieter the Elder (c.1515–69)/Musees Royaux des Beaux-Arts de Belgique, Brussels, Belgium, Giraudon/The Bridgeman Art Library **p.177** Time Transfixed, 1938 (oil on canvas) by Magritte, Rene (1898–1967) Art Institute of Chicago, IL. © ADAGP, Paris and DACS, London 2008 **p.182** Spring, (oil on canvas), Arcimboldo, Giuseppe (1527–93)/Private Collection, © Agnew's, London, UK/The Bridgeman Art Library; Summer, 1563, (oil on canvas), Arcimboldo, Giuseppe (1527–93)/Kunsthistorisches Museum, Vienna, Austria/The Bridgeman Art Library; Autumn, Arcimboldo, Giuseppe (1527–93)/Louvre, Paris, France, Lauros/Giraudon/The Bridgeman Art Library; Winter, (oil on canvas), Arcimboldo, Giuseppe (1527–93)/Kunsthistorisches Museum, Vienna, Austria/The Bridgeman Art Library **p.184** Joán Miró, Mural, March 20, 1961 Harvard University Art Museums, Fogg Art Museum, Gift of Mr. and Mrs. Josep Luis Sert, 1964.54 Copyright: Imaging Department © President and Fellows of Harvard College © Succession Miro/ADAGP, Paris and DACS, London 2008 **p.188** Portrait of Geoffrey Chaucer (1345–1400)/British Library, London, UK, © British Library Board. All Rights Reserved/The Bridgeman Art Library **p.189** Chaucer's Canterbury Pilgrims, engraved and pub. by the artist, 1810 (engraving), Blake, William (1757–1827) (after)/Private Collection/The Bridgeman Art Library **p.196** © Bettmann/CORBIS **p.199** The Art Archive/Tate Gallery London/Eileen Tweedy **p.205** John Clare by William Hilton, National Portrait Gallery, London **p.210** Portrait of Alfred, Lord Tennyson (1809–92) (b/w photo), Cameron, Julia Margaret (1815–79)/Private Collection, The Stapleton Collection/The Bridgeman Art Library **p.213** © 2003 Topham Picturepoint/Topfoto.co.uk **p.217** © Sotheby's/akg-images **p.224** Edward Gooch/Getty Images **p.231** © 2006 John Hedgecoe/Topfoto.co.uk **p.237** National Portrait Gallery, London **p.244** TopFoto/National News **p.247** Samuel Palmer Coming from Evening Church 1830 © Tate **p.248** National Portrait Gallery, London

Orders: please contact Bookpoint Ltd, 130 Milton Park, Abingdon, Oxon OX14 4SB. Telephone: (44) 01235 827720. Fax: (44) 01235 400454. Lines are open 9.00 – 5.00, Monday to Saturday, with a 24-hour message answering service. Visit our website at www.hoddereducation.co.uk

© Michael and Peter Benton 2008
First published in 2008 by
Hodder Education,
Part of Hachette Livre UK
338 Euston Road
London NW1 3BH

Impression number   10 9 8 7 6 5 4 3 2 1
Year   2013 2012 2011 2010 2009 2008

Cover photo NASA, ESA, J. Hester (ASU)
Illustrations by Barking Dog Art
Typeset in Gill Sans light 12pt by DC Graphic design Limited, Swanley Village, Kent.
Printed in Italy

A catalogue record for this title is available from the British Library

ISBN: 978 0340 96578 8

CONTENTS

Contents

iv

Part C Ten Poets 187

v

To the teacher

Touchstones Now is based on the following principles:

(1) That an anthology of poetry for pupils should have a generous *inclusiveness* which acknowledges that the poems pupils may enjoy, feel provoked by, remember and, maybe, find valuable are as likely to come from a performance script by John Agard or Michael Rosen as they are from a sonnet by Shakespeare.

(2) That *a mix of old and new poetry* is important. It is as misguided to think that what is 'relevant' to present-day pupils can only be poems written during their lifetime, as it is to promote the study of pre-twentieth century poetry merely on the grounds of its 'heritage' status.

(3) That the concept of a *teaching anthology*, developed through previous editions of this series, remains fundamental. The approaches we advocate are based on the premise that pupils' activities in reading and responding are the necessary preludes to their critical understanding of poetry.

(4) That *'creative' and 'critical' writing complement each other.* Learning by doing is a natural process with poems. All pupils have something to say: by channeling their ideas and feelings into making their own poems as well as into commentary – spoken and written – upon those of published poets, each informs the other.

Touchstones Now is in three parts. Part A introduces pupils to some basic technical and figurative devices and to different poetic forms. Part B presents ten themes through which pupils can explore similarities in subject matter, tone of voice, the expression of feelings and ideas, and formal features. Part C gives a representative sample of each of ten poet's work for pupils to gain a clear sense of the writer's style, cultural background, and way of looking at the world.

The anthology is fully supported by an interactive *Dynamic Learning Network CD-ROM* and a dedicated website. The *Dynamic Learning Network CD-ROM* contains interactive activities, videos, selected poetry readings and worksheets together with a comprehensive set of teaching notes.

Michael and Peter Benton
June 2008

PART

TEN

UNITS

A

Unit 1

PLAYING WITH WORDS

All poetry is playing with words. Writers play with letters, consonants and vowels; with sounds, rhythms and rhymes; with comparisons, associations and layout. All of these things may contribute to the meaning of a poem and to the picture that the words conjure up in our minds.

A poem might be light-hearted word-play, like a riddle or a nonsense verse, or it might be serious play in a poem about war or love or religion. Whatever the subject, the play with words aims to capture afresh a picture, a feeling or an idea so that we see or hear it in new ways.

Poems often make familiar things seem strange.

1 The Evening Star

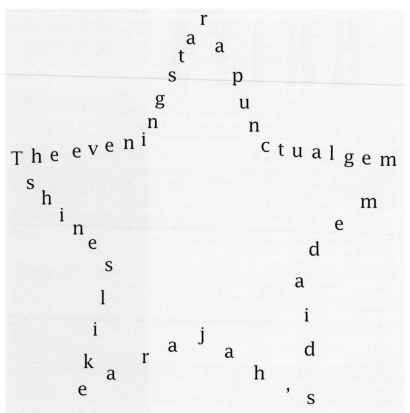

Guillaume Apollinaire

2

2 Tall Poplars in Stormy Weather

Green as the stream flows,
Flickering whipcord in the wind,
Lombardy thrashes.

Elisabeth

3

A bather whose clothing was strewed
By breezes that left her quite nude
   Saw a man walk along
   And, unless I am wrong,
You expect the last line to be rude.

Anon

4 Guitar

My neck is long
My sinew's Fine
strong my trunk
wood is made with No
arms, no toes
a bridge, no nose.
I may be a guitar-well
who knows? I fret, though
I am played with. How can
it be I have no eyes
yet I can C? How
is it that though
I am round I
can B flat?

Kevin Dickson

5

A pattern of waves
Across my bedroom curtains
Like a lazy sea.

John

6

My breast is puffed up and my neck is swollen.
I've a fine head and a high waving tail,
ears and eyes too, but only one foot;
a long neck, a strong beak, a back and
two sides, and a rod right through my middle.
My home is high above men. When he who moves
the forest molests me, I suffer a great deal of misery.
Scourged by the rainlash, I stand alone;
I'm bruised by heavy batteries of hail,
Hoar frost attacks and snow half-hides me.
I must endure all this, not pour out my misery.

Kevin Crossley-Holland

7

A tutor who tooted the flute
Tried to tutor two tooters to toot.
Said the two to the tutor,
'Is it harder to toot or
To tutor two tooters to toot?'

Anon

8

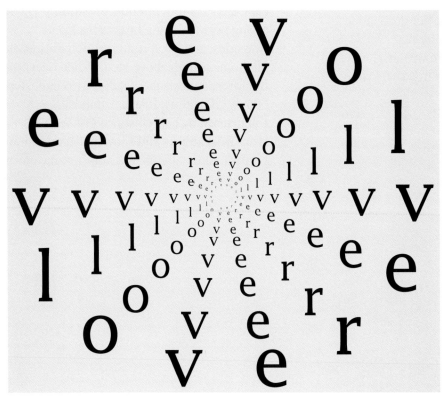

Alan Riddell

9

THE LOCH NESS MONSTER'S SONG

Edwin Morgan

Sssnnnwhufffll?
Hnwhuffl hhnnwfl hnfl hfl?
Gdroblboblhobngbl gbl gl g g g g glbgl.
Drublhaflablhaflubhafgabhaflhafl fl fl-
gm grawwwww grf grawf awfgm graw gm.
Hovoplodok-doplodovok-plovodokot-doplodokosh?
Splgraw fok fok splgrafhatchgabrlgabrl fok splfok!
Zgra kra gka fok!
Grof grawff gahf?
Gombl mbl bl-
blm plm,
blm plm,
blm plm,
blp.

10

HOW TO ADDRESS A GOLDFISH

Keith Bosley

O goldfish
O goldfish O
goldfish O goldfish
O goldfish O goldfish O
goldfish O goldfish O goldfish
O gold O fish OO gold O fish O
goldfish O goldfish O goldfish
O goldfish O goldfish O
goldfish O goldfish
O goldfish O
goldfish O

5

11 Amazed Cat

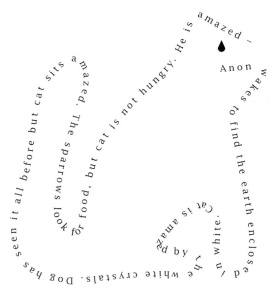

Anon

Activity 1

There are eight types of word-play in these poems. Work with a friend to find:

- **17-syllable poems**
- **Limericks**
- **Riddles**
- **Sound poems**
- **Tongue-twisters**
- Several varieties of pattern poetry:
  - **Silhouettes** (words arranged in the solid shape of their subject)
  - **Calligrams** (words tracing the outline of their subject)
  - **Concrete poems** (letters or words laid out to picture a poem's content).

Activity 2

- Have you solved the **riddle** in the poem *Here I Stand* (page **3**)? If not, read the poem again and ask 'What am I?'

- Make up your own riddle for an object you have chosen. You may find it helpful to use several of your senses. For example, think about what people would *see*, how it feels to *touch*, any *sound* it makes etc. Write in the first person: "I am …"

Activity 3

Haiku
The 17-syllable poems are called **haiku**, a Japanese word meaning 'word-picture'. We will look at this form in more detail in Unit 3, but for now we will think just about the syllable pattern.

- Look at the haiku, *Tall Poplars in Stormy Weather* (page **3**). Count and mark with a / the syllables in each line.

- When you are clear about the syllable pattern, choose your own word-picture and write a haiku for yourself.

Limericks
Limericks are funny, five-line poems where the longer lines (1, 2, and 5) rhyme with each other, as do the shorter lines (3 and 4). The longer lines usually have three heavy beats, and the shorter ones two heavy beats.

- As a group, read the limericks aloud.

- Make up a limerick of your own. Rhymes and rhythm are an important way of making a limerick humorous, so you may find it helpful to think of the first line to set the pattern and a punch line with which to finish. Then you can fill in the lines in between.

continued

Activity 3 – *continued*

Example:

/ / /

There was a young teacher from York   (line 1)

    /   /   /   (line 2)

    /   /   (line 3)

    /   /   (line 4)

    /   /   /

She threw out her whiteboard for chalk.   (line 5)

Possible rhymes for line 2 could be 'talk', 'walk', 'fork', 'hawk' etc. Brand new rhymes are needed for lines 3 and 4.

Concrete poems

Revolver is an example of a concrete poem where the writer arranges the letters of a word to suggest the meaning. A concrete poem is as much a picture as a poem.

- Look at the poem *Revolver* (page **4**) again. What does the layout of the letters suggest?

- Using *Revolver* as a model, choose a single word and arrange the letters into a concrete poem. What about using 'balloons', 'mirror', 'monsoon' or 'rocket'?

Activity 4

Performance

- As a class, practise reading *The Loch Ness Monster's Song* (page **5**). Where do you imagine the monster to be? What might he be doing? Vary the voices and the pace of your performance.

- Try writing another verse for the *Loch Ness Monster's Song*, using sounds you think are suitable.

Activity 5

Shapes

Silhouette poems

- Read the poem *Guitar* (page **3**). Take a simple shape for example, a square, circle, column, triangle, hand-outline, footprint, a light bulb, a bottle etc. Think what the shape suggests to you and find suitable words to fill it.

Calligrams

- Read *The Evening Star* or *Amazed Cat* and write your own calligram where the words fit the outline of the subject.

Unit 2
MAKING YOUR OWN NOTES AROUND A POEM

When we read a poem some parts may seem clear, others not so clear. There is often a lot packed into a small space and then it is useful to take a sort of mental walk around the poem to see how to get into it and how it can be unpacked.

It can be helpful to jot down your thoughts about a poem as you read it, logging your feelings and ideas by arranging them around the poem.

Cat

Sometimes I am an unseen
marmalade cat, the friendliest colour,
making off through a window without
    permission,
pacing along a broken-glass wall to the
    greenhouse,
jumping down with a soft, four-pawed thump,
finding two inches open of the creaking door
with the loose brass handle,
slipping impossibly in,
flattening my fur at the hush and touch of
    the sudden warm air,
avoiding the tiled gutter of slow green water,
skirting the potted nests of tetchy cactuses,
and sitting with my tail flicked
skilfully underneath me, to sniff
the azaleas   the azaleas   the azaleas.

Alan Brownjohn

Activity 1

Look carefully at how the sound and movement of the lines work together to create particular effects. As a group:

- Ring round **alliteration** and **assonance** in different colours and to ask yourself how they help you to picture the scene. Say the lines aloud. What feelings do they suggest?

- Underline words that keep up the sense of movement and ask why they are in the present tense.

- Look at the way the poem is punctuated and laid out on the page. How do these things guide your reading?

- What aspect of the cat is suggested by the repeated 'z' sound in the last line and the way the words 'the azaleas' are spaced out? Try reading it aloud.

- Which of the five senses (sight, sound, touch, smell and taste) are referred to in the poem?

When you have made your notes share them with the class.

After a homely cat here's a poem about an over-friendly rat.

Outside

Rats remember routes like ants.
That one you met, that grease-thighed
   monster,
knows the turns in your garden path,
ways through damp November earth,
has mapped in his mind the knots, the
   ladder
of your elaborate trellised creeper, noted
holds in the pockmarked brick and will
   return,
by claw on claw, to crouch and watch,
mimic, mock, hide in the screen of lacy
   steam
on the sill outside your bathroom window.

Whatsmore, next time you stretch and sigh,
reach one pink toe for the brass-look tap,
   spot
streaks on the glass, wire whiskers, teeth,
the red eyed stare, however much you
   shriek,
he'll only sleek one paw through slick
spiked fur and yawn. And even if you leap
or, rather, slip or squeak from the bath,
take a stand on your worn cork mat,
and, shaking, clap to scare him off,
the chances are that he'll clap back.

Kate Clanchy

Activity 2

- Read the poem *Outside*.

- Quickly write down your feelings and ideas by arranging them around the poem.

- How do you feel at the end?

- What is the story of the poem?

- Can you say why it makes you feel as you do?

Activity 3

Now look carefully at the way the poem develops:

- What does the first line suggest?

- What does the phrase 'grease-thighed monster' suggest?

- What is the effect of the long single sentence from line 2 to line 10?

- What is the effect of talking about 'your' bathroom window, not 'the' bathroom window?

- What is the writer's mood at the very beginning of the second section?

- How does it change? What is the rat's mood?

- The writer claps for one reason, the rat for another. What are they?

Unit 3

MAKING WORD-PICTURES

When we try to describe something in writing the right words don't always come and do not make the picture we want. It's difficult to give the shape of the idea in our heads the same 'shape' in words. Here are four ways of making 'word-pictures'.

Snapshots

A camera can take instant pictures of anything that catches your eye. Your mind can take quick snapshots too.

Activity 1

- Close your eyes and concentrate on a single word such as rat, stars, peace, rocks etc. It's best to choose a word that will set off lots of associations in your head. What ideas and pictures does the word conjure up? What thoughts does it link to? Apart from what you *see* in your mind's eye, what do your other senses – *hearing, touch, taste, smell* – tell you about what you see?

- When the picture in your mind's eye is clear enough, open your eyes and take your snapshot by jotting down as many words and phrases as you can to describe what you see. Do this quickly. Don't worry about spelling or making sentences for the moment. You could jot your ideas as a list or as a spider diagram if you prefer.

- Now compose your picture. Arrange your notes adding new words and crossing out ones you don't want. Try to make a two- or three-line snapshot.

- When you have made your words into a sharp image, write out a clean copy.

Haiku

A haiku poem is as brief and precise as a snapshot. Haiku poems are only three lines long and, because of their shortness, they cannot include a lot of detail. They may suggest a scene or an incident. They may create an atmosphere. They may express a person's feelings. They may do several of these things at the same time.

Activity 2

- Read these two translations of Japanese haiku poems:

Full Moon

Bright the full moon shines:
on the matting of the floor,
shadows of the pines.

Kikaku

Summer Night

A lightning flash:
Between the forest trees
I have seen water.

Shiki

These are clear, simple word-pictures in which the writer concentrates on one central object or scene and leaves the reader to imagine the details of the landscape.

- What other details of the picture do you see in your mind's eye when you read each of these poems? Describe the scene in each poem in your own words.

Haiku poems do not have to rhyme. The basic form is a seventeen-syllable poem, the syllables being arranged 5,7,5 over three lines. Here is a regular haiku written by a Key Stage 3 pupil:

Rain Haiku

Gentle summer rain   (5)
Scratch, scratch upon the window   (7)
With its little stick   (5)

Colin Rowbotham

Activity 3

- Try to write a regular haiku in the 5,7,5 pattern.

Activity 4

- Try writing a haiku sequence of, say, three poems to suggest your mood at different times of day, such as getting up, sitting in a lesson, coming home, or four poems for the seasons of the year, or twelve poems to make a haiku yearbook in which you catch the pictures of January, February, March and so on.
- Or, read through the following poem and see if you can add one or two other examples of 'housework haiku', e.g. on washing up or filling the dishwasher or dusting, making the bed, cooking etc.

Housework Haiku

I
The mirror is blurred.
I polish till it reflects
A room undisturbed.

II
The washing machine
Is conditioned to begin
Its neurotic spin.

III
Handwashing cotton
Connects me with the women
Time has forgotten.

IV
Instead of tea leaves,
Clairvoyants could have a laugh
With hairs in the bath.

V
The bin liner bursts,
Vomiting ever thicker
Cold chicken tikka.

VI
I am hypnotized
Ironing at massage speed
Yet another sleeve.

VII
The growling Hoover
Is very hungry to feed.
It strains on its lead.

VIII
I shall take a poll
To see how many people
Replace the loo roll.

Sarah Wardle

Thumbnail sketches

In these short, sketch-like haiku poems the reader has to fill out the picture by thinking round the few words that are given. Here is another word-picture (not a haiku this time) which suggests a good deal more than is written down.

In A Station of the Metro*   * The Paris underground

The apparition of these faces in the crowd;
Petals on a wet, black bough.

Ezra Pound

This poem was arrived at after a lot of work on a much longer version of the same idea. The poet's job was to prune away unnecessary words so that this finished poem would represent, in a sharp, uncluttered way, the experience of seeing a crowd of people in an underground station.

16

Activity 5

- What is the connection between the first line and the second of the poem above?
- Look up the word 'apparition'. Why does the poet use the word apparition rather than appearance?

Activity 6

- Write a few lines that capture as vividly and precisely as you can a scene that sticks in your mind. It could be anything, from a sunset to a football match. Whatever you choose, when you have the first draft of, say, five or six lines, try cutting away the unnecessary lines or phrases until you have two or three lines that say just what you want.

The bigger picture

In her poem *Legend*, Welsh poet Gillian Clarke recalls an incident from her childhood. It occurred in the great freeze of 1947 which was the snowiest winter for over 130 years. In many places it snowed almost every day for several weeks and there were snowdrifts over 2 metres deep. To get anywhere people had to use shovels to dig narrow paths with parapet walls of snow banked up on either side.

Activity 7

- Read the poem.
- With a friend, talk about what you think the story is.
- What words or phrases do you like most?
- What words or phrases help you to see that wintry world through her eyes and to make it real?

Legend

The rooms were mirrors
for that luminous face,
the morning windows ferned
with cold. Outside
a level world of snow.

Voiceless birds in the trees
like notes in the books
in the piano stool.
She let us suck top-of-the milk
burst from the bottles like corks.

Then wrapped shapeless
we stumped to the park
between parapets of snow
in the wake of the shovellers,
cardboard rammed in the tines* of garden forks.

*prongs

The lake was an empty rink
and I stepped out,
pushing my sister first
onto its creaking floor.
When I brought her home,

shivering, wailing, soaked,
they thought me a hero.
But I still wake at night,
to hear the Snow Queen's knuckles crack,
black water running fingers through the ice.

Gillian Clarke

Activity 8

The next poem is also by a Welsh writer, R.S. Thomas. Notice how he brings alive the picture of the farmer as he drives his new tractor proudly down the lane. Part of this sense of immediacy comes from the **metaphors**. We aren't told that his nerves are *like* metal or that he is *like* a knight at arms: we are told that his nerves *are* metal, that he *is* the knight at arms.

Cynddylan on a Tractor

Ah, you should see Cynddylan on a tractor.
Gone the old look that yoked him to the soil;
He's a new man now, part of the machine,
His nerves of metal and his blood oil.
The clutch curses, but the gears obey
His least bidding, and lo, he's away
Out of the farmyard, scattering hens.
Riding to work now as a great man should,
He is the knight at arms breaking the fields'
Mirror of silence, emptying the wood
Of foxes and squirrels and bright jays.
The sun comes over the tall trees
Kindling all the hedges, but not for him
Who runs his engine on a different fuel.
And all the birds are singing, bills wide in vain,
As Cynddylan passes proudly up the lane.

R.S. Thomas

- Look up the word 'yoke'. What do you think 'yoked to the soil' suggests about his life?

- How has the tractor changed Cynddylan?

- In Welsh history Cynddylan was a celebrated heroic king. What words suggest that farmer Cynddylan sees himself as kingly?

- How has his relationship with nature been altered by having a tractor?

Unit 4

COMPARISONS

We use comparisons all the time to express our feelings and to describe things more vividly. Here is an old poem that is simply a list of comparisons.

Comparisons

As wet as a fish — as dry as a bone;
As live as a bird — as dead as a stone;
As plump as a partridge — as poor as a rat;
As strong as a horse — as weak as a cat;
As hard as a flint — as soft as a mole;
As white as a lily — as black as a coal;
As plain as a staff — as rough as a bear;
As tight as a drum — as free as air;
As heavy as lead — as light as a feather;
As steady as time —uncertain as weather;
As hot as an oven — as cold as a frog;
As gay as a lark — as sick as a dog;
As savage as tigers — as mild as a dove;
As stiff as a poker — as limp as a glove;
As blind as a bat — as deaf as a post;
As cool as a cucumber — as warm as toast;
As flat as a flounder — as round as a ball;
As blunt as a hammer — as sharp as an awl*;   *pointed instrument used by carpenters
As brittle as glass — as tough as gristle;
As neat as a pin — as clean as a whistle;
As red as a rose — as square as a box;
As bold as a thief — as sly as a fox.

Anon

Activity 1

- Read the poem *Comparisons*.

Some of the phrases are now so common that we hardly think of them as comparisons. Over-used comparisons such as 'As light as a feather' are called **clichés**.

- Which comparisons do you recognise and which are new to you?
- Why do you think the unknown author put 'As weak as a cat' instead of the usual cliché, 'as weak as a kitten'? And why 'As dead as a stone' instead of the traditional 'As dead as a doornail'?
- What new comparisons can you think of instead of the rather tired old ones?

Two kinds of comparison

Here are two Japanese haiku poems that use comparisons:

In the Moonlight

It looks like a man,
the scarecrow in the moonlit night —
and it is pitiful.

Shiki

The Barleyfield

Up the barley rows,
stitching, stitching them together,
a butterfly goes.

Sora

The first poem makes a direct comparison: the scarecrow is *like* a man. The second poem *assumes* the comparison of the zig-zag movement of the butterfly, up the rows of crops, to be similar to the movement of someone stitching cloth together using a zig-zag stitch.

You may know these two types of comparison already as **simile** and **metaphor**. A simile is when we compare two things by saying one is *like* another. A metaphor is when we say one thing *is* another (although we know that really it isn't). Similes and metaphors help make poems more vivid and they also help poets to say more exactly what they mean.

You can see how appropriate it is to describe poems like these as 'word-pictures'. In fact, the haiku poets are doing in words what the artist is doing in this picture he called *The Great Wave*. It was created about 1825 by the Japanese artist Hokusai as one of a series of pictures of the snow-capped Mount Fuji.

Activity 2

- What is the object behind the raised prow in the background of the picture – a mountain or another wave?

- What does the falling spray remind you of?

continued

Activity 2 – *continued*

- What does the foaming crest of the wave look like?

- Write down the comparisons that your answers to each of these questions suggest.

Activity 3

Now choose one of the comparisons you have discussed and write a haiku of your own with the title *The Great Wave.*

Comparisons allow us to see the things being described more clearly. The next poet takes the simple subject of flies buzzing at the window glass of a hot room. With an acute eye for detail and an ear for sound, the poet uses metaphors to make the experience real. The writer is in Italy so he gives his poem an Italian title.

La Stanza delle* Mosche (The Room of the Flies)

*In Italian, 'stanza' means room or verse.

The room sizzles in the morning sun;
a tinnitus of flies at the bright windows,
butting and dunting the glass. One dings
off the light, to the floor, vibrating blackly,
pittering against the wall before taxi
and take-off — another low moaning flight,
another fruitless stab at the world outside.
They drop on my desk, my hands,
and spin their long deaths on their backs
on the white tiles, first one way
then the other, tiny humming tops that
stop and start: a sputter of bad wiring,
whining to be stubbed out.

Robin Robertson

Activity 4

What does each of these metaphors suggest?

1   The room **sizzles**...

2   a **tinnitus** of flies (tinnitus is the medical condition of *having a continual sensation of ringing or buzzing in the ears*)

3   before taxi/and take-off

4   tiny humming tops...

5   a sputter of bad wiring...

6   ...stubbed out.

Activity 5

- Read through the following comparisons. They are all extracts from longer poems apart from nos. 5 and 6 which are complete. As you read, give the words time to form a picture in your mind. Make notes to help you remember this picture. Then ask yourself:

- Which comparisons did you like?

- Which ones could you not see at all?

- Select your favourite extract and write a sentence saying what you like about the comparison, why it works for you.

1 Pigeons

Small blue busybodies
Strutting like fat gentlemen
With hands clasped
Under their swallowtail coats

Richard Kell

2 The Imprint of a Sea Shell on a Stone

And chiselled clear on stone
A spider-web of shell,
The thumb-print of the sea.

Norman Nicholson

3 A Donkey

His face is what I like.
And his head, much too big for his body
	— a toy head,
A great, rabbit-eared, pantomime head,
And his friendly rabbit face,
His big, friendly, humorous eyes —
	which can turn wicked,
Long and devilish, when he lays his ears
	back.

But mostly he's comical — and that's
	what I like.
I like the joke he seems
Always just about to tell me. And the
	laugh,
The rusty, pump-house engine that
	cranks up laughter
From some long-ago, far-off laughter-
	less desert —

The dry, hideous guffaw
That makes his great teeth nearly fall out.

Ted Hughes

continued

Activity 5 – *continued*

4 Snowflakes

Snowflakes
like tiny
insects
drifting
down.

John Agard

5 Boredom

Boredom
Is
Clouds
Black as old slate
Chucking rain straight
On our Housing Estate
All grey
Day long.

Gareth Owen

6 Cats

Cats are contradictions: tooth and claw
Velvet-padded;
Snowflake-gentle paw
A fist of pins;
Kettles on the purr
Ready to spit;
Black silk then bristled fur.

Phoebe Hesketh

Activity 6

- Re-read Phoebe Hesketh's picture of cats in extract 6. Three contradictory aspects of cats are described through comparisons in this short extract. The cat's paw, its purr and its fur are all seen in two different contradictory ways. Make a grid like this and fill in the right-hand column with words and phrases from the extract to show how they suggest the idea of cats as contradictions:

	One view	A different view
Cat's paw		
Cat's purr		
Cat's fur		

Activity 7

- As a group, choose your own subject, one that you could describe in several ways (a face, electricity pylons, inside a shop, The London Eye, a block of flats) and each of you make up one line or phrase, using a comparison to describe it. Sort out the best order for your lines, think of a title and write out a group poem.

Unit 5

RHYTHM AND MOVEMENT

Rhythm in poetry, as in music, is a kind of pattern that underlies and holds together the whole structure of a poem. Sometimes, as in music, the rhythm may be so strong that it is the most important part of the poem. Sometimes the rhythm is deliberately played down and is quiet and unnoticed.

Activity 1

- Read the poem *Woodpecker* by the poet John Agard and decide in groups how to present it as a group reading. There are several possible ways.

Woodpecker

Carving
tap/tap
music
out of
tap/tap
tree trunk
keep me
busy
whole day
tap/tap
long

tap/tap
pecker
birdsong
tap/tap
pecker
birdsong

tree bark
is tap/tap
drumskin
fo me beak
I keep
tap/tap
rhythm
fo forest
heartbeat

tap/tap
chisel beak
long
tap/tap
honey leak
song
pecker/tap
tapper/peck
pecker
birdsong

John Agard

28

A quite different rhythm and much deeper feeling underlies Edward Brathwaite's poem *Limbo* (page **30**). In a limbo dance the dancer sways backwards closer and closer to the ground and almost parallel to it so as to pass under a very low bar. The dance is a tourist attraction these days in the Caribbean where Brathwaite comes from, but it dates back to the days of slavery.

The poem reminds us of the foul and degrading conditions in which slaves were carried on the 100-day voyage from Africa to the Americas. The only way the chained slaves could exercise lying in the dark, stinking holds of the slave ships, often seasick and in their own excrement, was by moving in this cramped fashion. The diagram is one of several showing how slaves could be packed into every available space aboard ship.

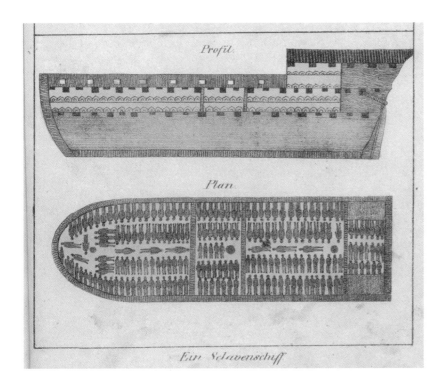

Activity 2

- Discuss this diagram of how a typical slave ship was loaded.
- Now read the poem *Limbo*.

Limbo

And limbo stick is the silence in front of me
limbo

limbo
limbo like me
limbo
limbo like me

long dark night is the silence in front of me
limbo
limbo like me

stick hit sound
and the ship like it ready

stick hit sound
and the dark still steady

limbo
limbo like me

long dark deck and the water surrounding
    me
long dark deck and the silence is over me

limbo
limbo like me

stick is the whip
and the dark deck is slavery

stick is the whip
and the dark deck is slavery

limbo
limbo like me

drum stick knock
and the darkness is over me

knees spread wide
and the water is hiding me

limbo
limbo like me

knees spread wide
and the dark ground is under me

down
down
down

and the drummer is calling me
limbo
limbo like me

sun coming up
and the drummers are raising me

out of the dark
and the dumb gods are raising me

up
up
up

and the music is saving me

hot
slow
step

on the burning ground.

Edward Kamau Brathwaite

Activity 3

- How does the poem and the movement of the dance echo the journey of the captive slaves from Africa, into the hold of the ship and finally to the end of their journey?

- The word 'Limbo' can also mean 'Oblivion: the state of being disregarded or forgotten'; it can mean 'A state or place of confinement' or 'An intermediate place or state'. How does each of these meanings relate to the poem and extend our first ideas of a simple limbo dance for the tourists?

Activity 4

- Prepare a dramatised reading of the poem, calling up different voices in turn. Try to let the haunting limbo rhythm, which is almost like a spell, speak through the poem.

On the next page, W.H. Auden's poem *The Quarry* tells of someone betrayed to the soldiers by a lover. Much of its power comes from its insistent rhythm and the repetitions that build up to the climax of the last verse. The drumming of the soldiers that opens the poem is kept in our minds as the story unfolds.

The word 'quarry' in the title means an animal (or, in this case, a person) to be hunted down as prey.

The Quarry

O what is that sound which so thrills the ear
Down in the valley drumming, drumming?
Only the scarlet soldiers, dear,
The soldiers coming.

O what is that light I see flashing so clear
Over the distance brightly, brightly
Only the sun on their weapons, dear,
As they step lightly.

O what are they doing with all that gear,
What are they doing this morning, this
    morning?
Only their usual manoeuvres, dear,
Or perhaps a warning.

O why have they left the road down there,
Why are they suddenly wheeling, wheeling?
Perhaps a change in their orders, dear,
Why are you kneeling?

O haven't they stopped for the doctor's care,
Haven't they reined their horses, their
    horses?
Why they are none of them wounded, dear,
None of these forces.

O is it the parson they want with white hair,
Is it the parson, is it, is it?
No, they are passing his gateway, dear,
Without a visit.

O it must be the farmer who lives so near.
It must be the farmer so cunning, so
    cunning?
They have passed the farmyard already, dear,
And now they are running.

O where are you going? Stay with me here!
Were the vows you swore deceiving,
    deceiving?
No, I promised to love you, dear,
But I must be leaving.

O it's broken the lock and splintered the
    door,
O it's the gate where they're turning, turning
Their boots are heavy on the floor
And their eyes are burning.

W.H. Auden

Activity 5

- Read the poem *The Quarry* together. In all but the last verse the first two lines of each verse are spoken by the person being hunted (the betrayed); the second two lines are spoken by the lover who betrays. The last verse is the victim's.

- Listen to two or three different readings of the poem. Talk about the images and the questions the poem leaves in your mind. What makes them so strong?

Activity 6

One of the liveliest rhythms is that of the 'galloping' poem. The two best-known examples are William Cowper's poem about John Gilpin's horse ride and Robert Browning's *How They Brought the Good News from Ghent to Aix*. Browning's poem begins:

x /   x   x   /   x x   / x x   /

I sprang to the stirrup, and Joris and he;
I galloped, Dirck galloped, we galloped all three;
'Good speed!' cried the watch, as the gate-bolts undrew;
'Speed!' echoed the wall to us galloping through;
Behind shut the postern*, the lights sank to rest,   *gate
And into the midnight we galloped abreast.

The heavy (**/**) and light (**x**) stresses are marked in line 1 to show you how the galloping rhythm works but you will hear it best by reading the lines aloud.

In the desperate ride that follows, only the storyteller reaches Aix. No one knows what the good news was. Browning seems more interested in the galloping rhythm! Perhaps the pointlessness of it all explains why the style has often been imitated as in the version which is entitled *How I Brought the Good News from Aix to Ghent (or Vice Versa)* which begins:

I sprang to the rollocks and Jorrocks and me,
And I galloped, you galloped, he galloped, we galloped all three...
Not a word to each other; we kept changing place,
Neck to neck, back to front, ear to ear, face to face;
And we yelled once or twice, when we heard a clock chime,
'Would you kindly oblige us, *Is that the right time?*' ...

R.J. Yeatman and W.C. Sellar

Activity 7

- Try to write a few 'galloping' lines of your own.

Not all rhythms have to be so complex, though. James Kirkup wrote this poem for a little baby and deliberately kept the rhythm very simple.

Baby's Drinking Song

For a baby learning for the first time to drink from a cup (Vivace*)   *Lively

> Sip a little
> Sup a little
>   From your little
> Cup a little
>   Sup a little
> Sip a little
>   Put it to your
> Lip a little
>   Tip a little
> Tap a little
>   Not into your
> Lap or it'll
>   Drip a little
> Drop a little
>   On the table
> Top a little.
>
>   *James Kirkup*

Activity 8

- What is the pattern of the rhythm here? Mark the heavy and the light stresses using **/** for heavy and **x** for light. Try tapping it out if you aren't sure.
- Why do you think the writer chose this pattern for this subject?

Dis Poetry
(from *City Psalms*)

Dis poetry is like a riddim dat drops
De tongue fires a riddim dat shoots like shots
Dis poetry is designed fe rantin
Dance hall style, big mouth chanting,
Dis poetry nar put yu to sleep
Preaching follow me
Like yu is blind sheep,
Dis poetry is not Party Political
Not designed fe dose who are critical.

Dis poetry is wid me when I gu to me bed
It gets into me dreadlocks
It lingers around me head
Dis poetry goes wid me as I pedal me bike
I've tried Shakespeare, respect due dere
But dis is de stuff I like.

Dis poetry is not afraid of going ina book
Still dis poetry need ears fe hear an eyes fe
    hav a look
Dis poetry is Verbal Riddim, no big words
    involved
An if I hav a problem de riddim gets it solved,
I've tried to be more romantic, it does nu
    good for me
So I tek a Reggae Riddim an build me poetry,
I could try be more personal
But you've heard it all before,
Pages of written words not needed
Brain has many words in store,
Yu could call dis poetry Dub Ranting
De tongue plays a beat
De body starts skanking*,
Dis poetry is quick an childish
Dis poetry is fe de wise an foolish,

Anybody can do it fe free,
Dis poetry is fe yu an me,
Don't stretch yu imagination
Dis poetry is fe de good of de Nation,
Chant,
In de morning
I chant
In de night
I chant
In de darkness
An under de spotlight,
I pass thru University
I pass thru Sociology
An den I got a dread degree
In Dreadfull Ghettology.
Dis poetry stays wid me when I run or walk
An when I am talking to meself in poetry
    I talk,
Dis poetry is wid me,
Below me an above,
Dis poetry's from inside me
It goes to yu
WID LUV.

Benjamin Zephaniah

*walking in reggae rhythm

Activity 9

- In the first section of 9 lines, what does Benjamin say that his poetry *is*, and what does he say it is *not*?

- In the third section, what does Benjamin see as the big advantage of what he calls Verbal riddim?

- What advantages does he see in not having his poetry as pages of written words, but in his heart and brain, and spoken out loud?

- Who is his poetry aimed at?

Unit 6

SOUND AND MOVEMENT

Nonsense sounds

Activity 1

SLITHY, MIMSY, UFFISH

- Slithy, Mimsy and Uffish. Three words you may not have come across before!

- Say them to yourself a few times.

- In pairs or groups decide what they might mean and quickly write down any ideas they might suggest or anything they might describe.

- Share your ideas with the rest of the class.

Lewis Carroll's nonsense poem *Jabberwocky* comes from his novel *Through the Looking Glass*. At first it was printed in Looking Glass (mirror) writing, then in the way we would normally see it. Whatever way we look at it though it is very strange!

- As you read the poem, listen to the strange sounds and see the pictures they conjure up in your imagination:

continued

Activity 1 – *continued*

Jabberwocky

'Twas brillig, and the slithy toves
    Did gyre and gimble in the wabe;
All mimsy were the borogoves,
    And the mome raths outgrabe.

'Beware the Jabberwock, my son!
    The jaws that bite, the claws that catch!
Beware the Jubjub bird, and shun
    The frumious Bandersnatch!'

He took his vorpal sword in hand;
    Long time the manxome foe he sought—
So rested he by the Tumtum tree,
    And stood awhile in thought.

And, as in uffish thought he stood,
    The Jabberwock, with eyes of flame,
Came whiffling through the tulgey wood,
    And burbled as it came!

One, two! One, two! And through and through
    The vorpal blade went snicker-snack!
He left it dead, and with its head
    He went galumphing back.

'And hast thou slain the Jabberwock?
    Come to my arms, my beamish boy!
O frabjous day! Callooh! Callay!'
    He chortled in his joy.

'Twas brillig, and the slithy toves
    Did gyre and gimble in the wabe;
All mimsy were the borogoves,
    And the mome raths outgrabe.

continued

Activity 1 – *continued*

- When she hears the poem, Alice says '...it's *rather* hard to understand... Somehow it seems to fill my head with ideas – only I don't know exactly what they are!' What ideas does the poem give you?

Lewis Carroll loved making up words like 'tulgey', 'frabjous' and borogoves'. In *Through the Looking Glass*, Humpty Dumpty explains to Alice the meaning of some of the words. He says that 'slithy' means 'lithe and slimy'. Of course, Humpty Dumpty's explanations are not the only possible ones. Did 'slithy' suggest something different to you?

- Some people today use words like 'ginormous' or 'fantabulous'. What two words are they packing into one when they do?

Three of the words invented by Lewis Carroll are now in the Oxford Dictionary: 'galumphing' they suggest is from 'gallop' and 'triumphant' and means 'to march exultingly with irregular bounding movements', and 'chortle' is a mixture of 'chuckle' and 'snort'.

- 'Frabjous' also appears. What does this word suggest to you?

- Write down and compare your ideas about the meanings of some of these strange words. How far do you agree? Are there certain similarities?

- Do you agree that the sound of words, even nonsense words, can suggest meaning and feelings to us?

Activity 2

- Work out your own dramatic reading of the poem that you can perform for others or record. There are many possible ways of approaching it. For example, you could work in groups of about six and read the first and last verses as a group, with two other voices reading the two parts in inverted commas and a narrator reading the middle three verses. Experiment! Add weird and wonderful sound effects if you like.

- If you are really adventurous you could add these two nonsense French and German versions of the first verse. Amazingly they sound quite convincing.

Il brilgue: les toves lubricilleux
Se gyrent en vrillant dans le guave.
Enmimés sont les gougebosqueux
Et le momerade horsgrave.   *(French)*

Es brillig war. Die schlichten Toven
Wirrten und wimmelten in Waben;
Und aller-mumsige Burggoven
Die mohmen Rath' ausgraben.   *(German)*

Activity 3

- Experiment with writing your own nonsense verse. You could write a sequel to *Jabberwocky*. The Jabberwock is only one of three possible attackers the hero has to face. Write your own poem about the meeting of a hero or heroine with either the Jubjub bird or the frumious Bandersnatch. Be careful not to use too many nonsense words: Lewis Carroll uses many more normal words and phrases than he does invented ones.

Sound and sense: maloomas and taketis

Activity 4

Read this description of somebody washing up a sticky porridge pan. It comes from a longer poem called *Sink Song*.

Scouring out the porridge pot.
　　Round and round and round!

Out with all the scraith and scoopery,
Lift the eely ooly droopery,
Chase the glubbery slobbery
　　gloopery
　　Round and round and round.

J.A. Lindon

There are several invented words here but, if you have ever washed up a porridge pan, you will know how well they describe the rubbery skin and the slimy strings of porridge and the sucking, slopping sounds. And, if you have never done any washing up, reading this gives you a good idea of what it feels like. The sounds suggest other associations and therefore feelings.

Here, the writer chooses words to sound like the thing he is describing. This is called **onomatopoeia**. We all of us use onomatopoeia when we use words like 'babble', 'boom', 'slurp' and 'squelch'.

- Make a list, in your groups, of as many words you can think of whose sound suggests their meaning – onomatopoeic words.

Activity 5

- Say these words in your head:

  malooma... taketi... malooma... taketi

- Copy these shapes and write down which one you think is the malooma and which is the taketi.

- As a class, do you agree or disagree which is which? Why do you think people chose as they did?

Activity 6

balloon   mushroom   icicle   snatch   oozing   vicious

picnic   lash   summer   tripping   puddle   blade

Here are twelve words. Sort them into three columns – one for 'maloomas', one for 'taketis' and one for any you can't agree on.

Maloomas	Taketis	? Not sure

- Compare your lists with those of others.
- How did you decide which words to put in each list?
- Did you find some words more difficult to classify than others? If so, why?

Your lists show how some words suggest different qualities by their sounds and by their associations. These may not only be 'malooma' qualities of, for example, roundness or softness or 'taketi' qualities of sharpness and quickness, but also such things as warmth or coldness, lightness or heaviness.

UNIT 7

PATTERNS ON THE PAGE

Poems come in all shapes and sizes: fat ones and thin ones, long ones and short ones, ones that rhyme and ones that don't, and poems set out in various shapes as we saw in Unit 1.
This unit introduces four much used forms. Rhyme matters
a great deal in the first three – the couplet, the ballad and the sonnet, but is missing altogether in the fourth – free verse.

Couplets

A couplet is a pair (a 'couple') of lines, usually of the same length, that rhyme with each other. In the two examples below, one expresses gentleness of feeling whilst the other makes a witty joke.

Motherless Baby

Motherless baby and babyless mother
Bring them together to love one another

Christina Rossetti

This Englishwoman

This Englishwoman is so refined
She has no bosom and no behind.

Stevie Smith

Activity 1

- With Stevie Smith's couplet as your model, write your own rhyming couplet. You might start:

  This Englishman is such... (or 'is so')

  or

  This teacher talks so...

Couplets are often put together to tell stories. Here are two more examples. The first is based upon the book *Gulliver's Travels*, where Lemuel Gulliver is shipwrecked and finds himself in the land of Lilliput as a giant among tiny people only a few inches tall. The second (page **47**), is a modern poem which, with its dark humour, undermines the usual feelings between grandmother, mother and baby and reminds us of a number of horror films.

continued

Activity 1 – *continued*

Gulliver in Lilliput

From his nose
Clouds he blows.
When he speaks,
Thunder breaks.
When he eats,
Famine threats.
When he treads
Mountains' heads
Groan and shake;
Armies quake.
See him stride
Valleys wide,
Over woods,
Over floods.
Troops take heed,
Man and steed:
Left and right.
Speed your flight!
In amaze
Lost I gaze
Toward the skies
See! And believe your eyes!

Alexander Pope

Activity 2

- Read the poem *Gulliver in Lilliput*.
- Add one or two couplets:
  - 'When he cries...'
  - 'When he snores...'

Infant Song

Don't you love my baby, mam,
Lying in his little pram,

Polished all with water clean,
The finest baby ever seen?

> *Daughter, daughter, if I could*
> *I'd love your baby as I should,*
>
> *But why the suit of signal-red,*
> *The horns that grow out of his head,*
>
> *Why does he burn with brimstone heat,*
> *Have cloven hooves instead of feet,*
>
> *Fishing hooks upon each hand,*
> *The keenest tail that's in the land,*
>
> *Pointed ears and teeth so stark*
> *And eyes that flicker in the dark?*

Don't you love my baby, mam?

> *Dearest, I do not think I can.*
> *I do not, do not think I can.*

> *Charles Causley*

Activity 3

- With a friend, rehearse a reading of *Infant Song*, sharing out the lines between two voices.

The ballad

Ballads are narrative poems (they tell a story) and, centuries ago, were often sung by wandering minstrels who would accompany their songs on the harp. The next unit tells you more about this form and how it has developed in more recent times. Here, to introduce you to the form, is a medieval ballad — a tale about treachery and greed in a serial killer who finally gets his just desserts.

The Outlandish Knight

An outlandish* knight came out of the North   *foreign
  To woo a maiden fair,
He promised to take her to the North lands,
  Her father's only heir.

"Come, fetch me some of your father's gold,
  And some of your mother's fee*;   *property, money
And two of the best nags out of the stable,
  Where they stand thirty and three."

She fetched him some of her father's gold
  And some of her mother's fee
And two of the best nags out of the stable,
  Where they stood thirty and three.

She mounted her on her milk-white steed,
  He on the dapple grey;
They rode till they came unto the sea-side,
  Three hours before it was day.

"Light off, light off thy milk-white steed,
  And deliver it unto me;
Six pretty maids have I drowned here,
  And thou the seventh shall be.

"Pull off, pull off thy silken gown,
  And deliver it unto me;
Methinks it looks too rich and too gay*   * brightly coloured and showy
  To rot in the salt sea.

"Pull off, pull off thy silken stays,*   * bodice
  And deliver them unto me;
Methinks they are too fine and gay
  To rot in the salt sea.

"Pull off, pull off thy Holland smock*   * linen chemise
  And deliver it unto me:
Methinks it is too rich and gay
  To rot in the salt sea."

"If I must pull off my Holland smock,
  Pray turn thy back unto me,
For it is not fitting that such a ruffian
  A woman unclad should see."

He turned his back towards her,
  And viewed the leaves so green;
She caught him round the middle so small,
  And tumbled him into the stream.

He dropped high, and he dropped low,
  Until he came to the tide –
"Catch hold of my hand my pretty maiden,
  And I will make you my bride."

"Lie there, lie there, you false-hearted man,
  Lie there instead of me;
Six pretty maidens have you drowned here,
  And the seventh hath drowned thee."

She mounted on her milk-white steed,
  And led the dapple grey.
She rode till she came to her father's hall
  Three hours before it was day.

Anon

Activity 4

- Ballads are usually in simple language and often have clear images that may be repeated several times as well as repeated phrases. Can you find examples of these?
- Ballads are usually written in four-line verses with a variety of rhyming patterns. What is the rhyme scheme in this one?

The sonnet

A sonnet is a poem of 14 lines usually divided into 8 and 6 lines (the **octave** and the **sestet**) and with a regular rhyme scheme. There are often five light stresses (marked **x**) and 5 heavy stresses (marked **/**) to each line — like repeating the word 'again' five times. For example, the first line of the famous war poem, *The Soldier* is:

x /   x   /   x   / x /   x   /
If I should die, think only this of me:

In practice, both the rhymes and the rhythms vary a lot from poem to poem according to the subject matter. The poem below is one of many by John Clare which show his love and knowledge of the natural world. (You will find more poems and information about the poet on page **207**.)

The Thrush's Nest

Within a thick and spreading hawthorn bush,
That overhung a molehill large and round,
I heard from morn to morn a merry thrush
Sing hymns to sunrise, and I drank the sound
With joy; and, often an intruding guest,
I watched her secret toils from day to day —
How true she warped the moss to form a nest,
And modelled it within with wood and clay;
And, by and by, like heath-bells gilt with dew,
There lay her shining eggs, as bright as flowers,
Ink-spotted-over shells of greeny blue;
And there I witnessed in the sunny hours
A brood of nature's minstrels chirp and fly,
Glad as that sunshine and the laughing sky.

John Clare

Activity 5

Notice how the poem moves from the poet's first hearing of the thrush's song through several later visits to the hawthorn bush. Notice too, that although the poem is all one sentence, after line 8 the focus of the poem shifts. You are most aware of this when you hear the poem read aloud.

- On a separate copy of the poem, mark off in different colours the four main phases that the poem describes: discovering where the thrush was singing; building the nest; finding the eggs; the chirping and first flight of the newly-hatched young.

- Using the letters A to G show the rhyme scheme of the sonnet by putting the appropriate letter at the end of each of the 14 lines.

Composed Upon Westminster Bridge, September 3, 1802

Earth has not any thing to show more fair:
Dull would he be of soul who could pass by
A sight so touching in its majesty:
This City now doth, like a garment, wear
The beauty of the morning; silent, bare,
Ships, towers, domes, theatres, and temples lie
Open unto the fields, and to the sky;
All bright and glittering in the smokeless air.
Never did sun more beautifully steep
In his first splendour, valley, rock, or hill;
Ne'er saw I, never felt, a calm so deep!
The river glideth at his own sweet will:
Dear God! The very houses seem asleep;
And all that mighty heart is lying still!

William Wordsworth

Free verse

Free verse poetry is only free in the sense of not making use of rhyme or **metre**, or of traditional forms such as the three above. Instead it is controlled by the moods and meanings of the writer: the organisation of the poem, its sections and line lengths, follow the needs of the content, rather than having the content fitted into a predetermined form. So free verse is not formless. In fact, in the best examples, as in the poem below, the form becomes part of the meaning.

In the poem *Bat*, D.H. Lawrence recalls an evening in Italy when he was watching swallows flying beneath the arches of the Ponte Vecchio, the ancient bridge over the River Arno in Florence. Suddenly he realises that he is not watching swallows any longer but that bats have taken their place.

Bat

At evening, sitting on this terrace,
When the sun from the west, beyond Pisa, beyond
    the mountains of Carrara
Departs, and the world is taken by surprise...

When the tired flower of Florence is in gloom beneath the
    glowing
Brown hills surrounding...
When under the arches of the Ponte Vecchio
A green light enters against stream, flush from the west,
Against the current of obscure Arno...

Look up, and you see things flying
Between the day and the night;
Swallows with spools of dark thread sewing the shadows
    together.

A circle swoop, and a quick parabola under the bridge arches
Where light pushes through;
A sudden turning upon itself of a thing in the air.
A dip to the water.

And you think:
'The swallows are flying so late!'

Swallows?

Dark air-life looping,
Yet missing the pure loop...
A twitch, a twitter, an elastic shudder in flight
And serrated wings against the sky,
Like a glove, a black glove thrown up at the light,
And falling back.

Never swallows!
Bats!
The swallows are gone.

At a wavering instant the swallows give way to bats
By the Ponte Vecchio...
Changing guard.

Bats, and an uneasy creeping in one's scalp
As the bats swoop overhead!
Flying madly.

Pipistrello!
Black piper on an infinitesimal pipe.
Little lumps that fly in air and have voices indefinite, wildly vindictive;

Wings like bits of umbrella.

Bats!

Creatures that hang themselves up like an old rag to sleep;
And disgustingly upside down.
Hanging upside down like rows of disgusting old rags
And grinning in their sleep.
Bats!

In China the bat is a symbol of happiness.

Not for me!

D.H. Lawrence

Activity 6

Long lines and short lines

- Each of the first three sections has a line that is so long it spills over into inset words underneath. What do you notice about the movement and word-sounds of these lines?

- How does the length of the lines work with these things to create a mood?

- The shortest lines are just one or two isolated words, often with an exclamation mark. Why?

Structure

- Instead of verses the poem is made up of 15 irregular sections. How does this structure reflect the poet's changing mood and feelings towards the creatures he describes?

Comparisons

- Choose two or three examples of similes and metaphors you like that seem to capture the movements and appearance of the two creatures. Describe the pictures that the comparisons make in your mind's eye.

UNIT 8
BALLADS

Activity 1

- Read through this introduction to ballads and answer the questions.

Ballads of all sorts

What are ballads?

These stories in verse have been popular for hundreds of years and many of them survive today as folk songs. Ballads have always had strong connections with music. The early ballads were composed not as poems to be read but as songs to be sung or danced or even worked to. Ballads are usually simple in their language, often have very clear images such as 'milk-white steed', 'yellow hair' and frequently have a chorus or repeated line.

How and why were they made?

The earliest ballads date from a time when most people could not read or write and when there were no books available to most people. Ballads were a way of spreading news or opinions and, of course, of entertaining people.

What are they about?

Ballads were about many things – tales of adventure, of murder and scandal, religion and simply daily life. Some warned against various dangers. Some told tales of the ghosts, such as *The Unquiet Grave*. A few ballads on Christian subjects have been preserved into the present day as carols. *The Cherry-tree Carol* and *Mother and Maiden* are two of the best.

Work songs

People who work at repetitive tasks often sing to pass the time and to take their minds off the monotony of the job. In the past such tasks as spinning and weaving, grinding and mowing, ploughing the fields and rocking the cradle were all part of the daily routine and could be helped along by songs. Singing ballads helped sailors, for example, to keep time in tasks such as winding up the ship's anchor and hauling up the sails.

- What are sailors' ballads usually called?

Sensational stories

About 400 years ago a new kind of ballad developed. Booksellers and printers realised that sensational accounts of robberies, murders and hangings were very popular and soon ballads of this kind were printed and sold by the thousand. Travelling pedlars and street ballad-mongers made their living by them and to sell more copies they concentrated on crime, violence and scandal. For example, as late as 1849 the ballad about the murder of a man named Rush sold 2,500,000 copies.

The OLD BALLAD-SINGER.

- What was the new development that put such ballad mongers out of business and took the place of these scandal sheets?

Ballads today

Ballads did not die out because people like a good story. Many popular songs still use ballad form. Folk songs, work songs and carols continue to be written and poets continue to write ballad poems. In music you can find rock ballads, modern folk ballads, country and western ballads and so on. Look at the words of one or two recent songs that tell a story in ballad form. Share your findings with the class.

Activity 2

Performing a ballad 1

The Two Sisters of Binnorie is a dramatic story of love, jealous rivalry between sisters, murder and ghostly retribution. Compare it to some soap opera plots. The ballad can be read by the whole class, particularly if everyone joins in the repeated chorus lines which are in italics (they can be said in every verse). You will need a narrator (who does most of the reading), two sisters and a miller's son to make up the cast.

The Two Sisters of Binnorie

There were two sisters sat in a bower;
    Binnorie, O Binnorie;
There came a knight to be their wooer;
    By the bonny mill dams of Binnorie.

He courted the eldest with gloves and rings,
But he loved the youngest above all things,

The eldest was vexed to despair,
And much envied her sister fair.

The eldest said to the youngest one,
"Will ye see our father's ships come in?"

She's taken her by the lily-white hand,
And led her down to the river strand.

The youngest stood upon a stone;
The eldest came and pushed her in.

"O sister, sister reach your hand,
And you shall be heir of half my land.

"O sister, reach me but your glove
And sweet William shall be your love."

"Sink on, nor hope for hand or glove!
Sweet William shall surely be my love."

Sometimes she sank, sometimes she swam,
Until she came to the mouth of the dam.

Out then came the miller's son
And saw the fair maid swimming in.

"O father, father, draw your dam!
Here's either a mermaid or a swan."

The miller hasted and drew his dam,
And there he found a drowned woman.

You could not see her middle small,
Her girdle was so rich withal.

You could not see her yellow hair
For the gold and pearls that clustered there.

continued

Activity 2 – *continued*

And by there came a harper fine
Who harped to nobles when they dine.

And when he looked that lady on,
He sighed and made a heavy moan.

He's made a harp of her breast bone,
Whose sounds would melt a heart of stone.

He's taken three locks of her yellow hair
And with them strung his harp so rare.

He went into his father's hall
To play his harp before them all.

But as he laid it on a stone,
The harp began to play alone.

And soon the harp sang loud and clear,
"Farewell, my father and mother dear.

"Farewell, farewell, my brother Hugh,
    Farewell, my William, sweet and true."

And then as plain as plain could be,
    (Binnorie, O Binnorie)
"There sits my sister who drowned me
    By the bonny mill dams of Binnorie!"

Anon

57

Activity 3

Performing a ballad 2

The ballad of *Sir Patrick Spens* supposedly tells a story about the king of Scotland being persuaded to send Sir Patrick on a dangerous sea journey, in bad weather, to bring back the daughter of the king of Norway in 1285. Little is known about the real events and, as the ballad was printed five hundred years after they were supposed to have taken place, it may all be fiction.

Sir Patrick Spens

The king sits in Dunfermline town
        Drinking the blood-red wine:
'O where will I get a good sailor,
        To sail this ship of mine?'

continued

Activity 3 – *continued*

Up and spake an elder knight,
     Sat at the king's right knee:
'Sir Patrick Spens is the best sailor
     That ever sailed the sea.'

The king has written a braid* letter   *long
     And sealed it with his hand.
And sent it to Sir Patrick Spens
     Was walking on the strand.

'To Noroway, to Noroway,
     To Noroway o'er the foam;
The king's own daughter of Noroway
     'Tis thou must bring her home!'

The first line that Sir Patrick read
     A loud, loud laugh laughed he:
The next line that Sir Patrick read
     The tear blinded his ee.*   *eye

'O who is this has done this deed,
     This ill deed unto me;
To send me out this time o' the year
     To sail upon the sea?

'Make haste, make haste, my merry men all,
     Our good ship sails in the morn.'
'O say not so, my master dear,
     For I fear a deadly storm.

'I saw the new moon late yestere'en
     With the old moon in her arm;
And if we go to sea, master,
     I fear we'll come to harm.'

They had not sailed a league, a league,
     A league, but barely three,
When the sky grew dark, the wind blew loud,
     And angry grew the sea.

continued

Activity 3 – *continued*

The anchor broke, the topmast split,
     'Twas such a deadly storm.
The waves came over the broken ship
     Till all her sides were torn.

O long, long may the ladies sit
     With their fans into their hand
Or ere they see Sir Patrick Spens
     Come sailing to the strand.

O long, long may the maidens stand
     With their gold combs in their hair,
Before they'll see their own dear loves
     Come home to greet them there.

O forty miles off Aberdeen
     'Tis fifty fathoms deep,
And their lies good Sir Patrick Spens
     With the Scots lord at his feet.

Anon

- Prepare a group performance of the ballad. Think carefully who is speaking and what their feelings are likely to be. There are several different ways of splitting up the verses between different readers such as the voice of a narrator, the king, Sir Patrick Spens etc.

Making a ballad

Activity 4

Here are a few simple guidelines and an example to help you to write your own ballad. It is probably best to work in pairs.

- Agree on a story. Battles, disasters, ghosts are all common in older ballads. You can choose more modern topics such as a football match, a school trip full of incidents or the plot of a soap opera.

- Work out a story plan for about six verses. Keep it simple. Make sure your story has a beginning, middle and end.

- Read through several ballads and listen particularly to the rhythms and rhymes. A common pattern is to have a four-line verse in which lines 1 and 3 are longer than the others and where lines 2 and 4 rhyme.

- Decide on the pattern that sounds best to you and write your first verse. If you get stuck, don't worry. Leave a gap and try a later verse in your story plan.

Here is an example of a modern ballad written by a Key Stage 3 pupil.

The Ballad of Bovver Pete

In a house
On Windblown Street,
Lived a boy
Called bovver Pete.

He wore big boots
Upon his feet,
A real tough nut
Was bovver Pete.

He'd go out all day
Walking tall,
And practise bovver
On a hard brick wall.

His head was hard
As hard as brick,
He was very tough
But also thick.

Yes bovver Pete
Man he was tough,
But he met his match
In Jim Macduff.

Now bovver Pete
He picked a fight,
With Jim Mcduff
One winter's night.

Now bovver Pete
He gave him nuts,
And quickly followed
With a few head-butts.

Now Jim got angry
Took out his blade,
And Pete now became
Just second-grade.

Now Pete he slowly
Backed away.
He wanted to live
Till another day.

But Jim struck quick
His knife felt blood.
And Pete did fall
In the filthy mud.

Now bovver Pete
He's gone up top,
To the skinhead club
And the bovver shop.

Now everyone will remember Pete,
And take off their hats and say:
He wasn't really all that bad
In his own sorta way.

Efstathios

What has Happened to Lulu?

What has happened to Lulu, mother?
    What has happened to Lu?
There's nothing in her bed but an old rag doll
    And by its side a shoe.

Why is her window wide, mother,
    The curtain flapping free,
And only a circle on the dusty shelf
    Where her money-box used to be?

Why do you turn you head, mother,
    And why do the tear drops fall?
And why do you crumple that note on the fire
    And say it is nothing at all?

I woke to voices late last night,
    I heard an engine roar.
Why do you tell me the things I heard
    Were a dream and nothing more?

I heard somebody cry, mother,
    In anger or in pain,
But now I ask you why, mother,
    You say it was a gust of rain.

Why do you wander about as though
    You don't know what to do?
What has happened to Lulu, mother?
    What has happened to Lu?

Charles Causley

Activity 5

- Read the poem.

- Decide what you think has happened to Lulu.

- Discuss what you imagine is the state of mind of the three characters – the younger child who asks the questions, the mother, the missing Lulu. What evidence do you have? Share your ideas with the rest of the class and then read the poem again.

Unit 9

WORD PICTURES AND IDEAS

Pictures into ideas

How do you write a poem about a rainbow without mentioning any of its colours?
Like this!

Rainbow

When you see
de rainbow
you know
God know
wha he doing –
one big smile
across the sky –
I tell you
God got style
the man got style

When you see
raincloud pass
an de rainbow
make a show
I tell you
is God doing
limbo
the man doing
limbo

But sometimes
you know
when I see
de rainbow
so full of glow
and curving
like she bearing child
I does want to know
if God
ain't a woman

If that is so
the woman got style
man she got style

John Agard

63

Activity 1

- Rehearse one or two readings of the poem, perhaps sharing the sections between several readers.

- What do you make of the idea in the third section?

Ideas into pictures

Poets often use **personification** when they want to express an abstract idea. You will see from this word-picture that personification means turning an abstract idea such as 'love' or 'fear' into an imaginary person. Here is Edmund Spenser's personification of *Gluttony* (the deadly sin of excessive eating) written 400 years ago.

Gluttony

And by his side rode loathsome *Gluttony*,
    Deformed creature on a filthy swine,
    His belly was up-blow with luxury,
    And eke* with fatness swollen were his eyne.   *also
    And like a crane his neck was long and fine.
    With which he swallowed up excessive feast,
    For want whereof poor people oft did pine,
    And all the way, most like a brutish beast,
He spewéd up his gorge*, that all did him deteast.   *vomited up what he
                                         had swallowed

In green vine leaves he was right fitly clad*;   *suitably dressed
    For other clothes he could not wear for heat,
    And on his head an ivy garland had,
    From under which fast trickled down the sweat;
    Still as he rode, he somewhat still did eat,
    And in his hand did bear a boozing can,
    Of which he supped so oft, that on his seat
    His drunken corpse* he scarce upholden can,   *body
In shape more like a monster than a man.

Edmund Spenser

Activity 2

- Talk about the picture of this character that you get in your mind's eye.
- Select two or three details from the poem and then draw what your mind's eye sees. Title your drawing 'Personification'.

Words in action

In the next poem, Ted Hughes gives us a gale force wind at full blast. Rhythm, movement, word sounds and comparisons are all in action here.

Wind

This house has been far out at sea all night,
The woods crashing through darkness, the booming hills,
Winds stampeding the fields under the window
Floundering black astride and blinding wet

Till day rose; then under an orange sky
The hills had new places, and wind wielded
Blade-light, luminous black and emerald,
Flexing like the lens of a mad eye.

At noon I scaled along the house-side as far as
The coal-house door. Once I looked up —
Through the brunt wind that dented the balls of my eyes
The tent of the hills drummed and strained its guyrope,

The fields quivering, the skyline a grimace,
At any second to bang and vanish with a flap:
The wind flung a magpie away and a black-
Back gull bent like an iron bar slowly. The house

Rang like some fine green goblet in the note
That any second would shatter it. Now deep
In chairs, in front of the great fire, we grip
Our hearts and cannot entertain book, thought,

Or each other. We watch the fire blazing,
And feel the roots of the house move, but sit on,
Seeing the window tremble to come in,
Hearing the stones cry out under the horizons.

Ted Hughes

Activity 3

- Make your own jottings around a copy of the poem about such things as phrases you like, words or ideas you don't understand, feelings the description gives you, pictures in your mind's eye and so on. Your notes might look something like this:

Not really; metaphor.
House like ship in a storm

This house has been <u>far out at sea</u> all night,

The woods <u>crashing</u> through darkness, the <u>booming</u> hills,

Onomatapoeia, Sound echoes meaning.

Lots of active verbs suggest gale-force winds happening NOW

Winds stampeding the fields under the window

Floundering <u>black astride</u> and blinding wet

??? means?

These are a few things you could say about the first verse. Continue with your own notes for the rest of the poem.

- Share what each of you has found out about the poem.

Activity 4

Look back at your own notes on the poem. Choose the phrases you think best express the idea of the wind. Write a *Wind Haiku* using your own and, if it helps, Ted Hughes' words.

Word pictures and ideas

Here are some more poems in which particular ideas are suggested through creating a word-picture. What is the main idea behind each of the word-pictures?

Precious Stones

An emerald is as green as grass;
  A ruby red as blood;
A sapphire shines as blue as heaven;
  A flint lies in the mud.

A diamond is a brilliant stone,
  To catch the world's desire;
An opal holds a fiery spark;
  But a flint holds fire.

Christina Rossetti

'I Wandered Lonely as a Cloud'

I wandered lonely as a Cloud
That floats on high o'er Vales and Hills,
When all at once I saw a crowd,
A host of golden daffodils;
Beside the lake, beneath the trees,
Fluttering and dancing in the breeze.

Continuous as the stars that shine
And twinkle on the milky way,
They stretched in never-ending line
Along the margin of a bay:
Ten thousand saw I at a glance,
Tossing their heads in sprightly dance.

The waves beside them danced, but they
Out-did the sparkling waves in glee:
A poet could not but be gay
In such a jocund* company: *light-hearted, joyful
I gazed—and gazed—but little thought
What wealth the show to me had brought:

For oft when on my couch I lie
In vacant or in pensive* mood,   *filled with sad thoughts
They flash upon that inward eye
Which is the bliss of solitude,
And then my heart with pleasure fills,
And dances with the Daffodils.

William Wordsworth

67

Sindhi* Woman

* from Sind region and speaks
  Sindhi language

Barefoot through the bazaar*,
and with the same undulant* grace
as the cloth blown back from her face,
she glides with a stone jar
high on her head
and not a ripple in her tread.

*market
*swaying

Watching her cross erect
stones, garbage, excrement, and crumbs
of glass in the Karachi* slums,
I, with my stoop, reflect
they stand most straight
who learn to walk beneath a weight.

*major city in Pakistan

Jon Stallworthy

Summary of a Western

We see a dusty desert scene and that's
The way the film begins. Some men in hats
Deliver gritty lines. They all wear braces.
They're cool and tough. They hate the darker races
Who paint peculiar stripes across their faces.

Goodies meet baddies, mostly in corrals.
Cowboys ignore or patronize their gals.
We see a gun twirl in a macho hand.
Who's killing whom we don't quite understand —
There's always some vague reference to the land.

Women in aprons have to be protected.
Stagecoaches fall. New sheriffs are elected.
The cast consists primarily of horses —
They gallop to the ending, which of course is
A happy one, where nobody divorces.

Sophie Hannah

Sepia Fashion Show

Their hair, pomaded, faces jaded
bones protruding, hip-wise,
The models strutted, backed and butted,
Then stuck their mouths out, lip-wise.

They'd nasty manners, held like banners,
while they looked down their nose-wise,
I'd see 'em in hell, before they'd sell
me one thing they're wearing, clothes-wise.

The Black Bourgeois, who all say "yah"
When yeah is what they're meaning
Should look around, both up and down
before they set out preening.

 "Indeed" they swear, "that's what I'll wear
When I go country-clubbing."
I'd remind them please, look at those knees
you got at Miss Ann's scrubbing.

Maya Angelou

Activity 5

- Read through the poems. Choose one and write two sentences, one to describe the picture created in your mind's eye by the poem, and the other to say what you think is the main idea the poem expresses.

- Discuss your ideas with other members of the group.

UNIT 10
MIXED FEELINGS

Pictures of feelings

Negative feelings, positive feelings, mixed feelings — this unit looks at a few poems which explore different feelings. Haiku poems are a good place to start because their smallness means that they usually focus upon a single feeling.

In the following haiku poems we see a scene in our mind's eye and know what the writer feels:

In the House

At the butterflies
the caged bird gazes, envying —
just watch its eyes!

Issa

Parting

For me who go,
for you who stay —
two autumns.

Buson

Activity 1

- In the first poem, what are the feelings of the caged bird? Why does the poet refer to its eyes?

- In *Parting,* what is the feeling expressed by the phrase 'two autumns'?

In his poem *The Mesh*, the Ghanaian poet Kwesi Brew captures a similar feeling to that of *Parting*.

The Mesh

We have come to the cross-roads
And I must either leave or come with you.
I lingered over the choice
But in the darkness of my doubts
You lifted the lamp of love
And I saw in your face
The road that I should take.

Kwesi Brew

Activity 2

- What three images does Kwesi Brew use to convey how he is feeling?
- What decision do you think he makes? Why?
- Why do you think he gave his poem the title *The Mesh*?

Hurt No Living Thing

Hurt no living thing;
Ladybird nor butterfly,
Nor moth with dusty wing,
Nor cricket chirping cheerily,
Nor grasshopper so light of leap,
Nor dancing gnat, nor beetle fat,
Nor harmless worms that creep.

Christina Rossetti

Activity 3

- Read the poem above.
- The poem begins with an idea in line 1 and then illustrates it with a list of creatures. Why do you think the poet chooses only tiny and, some might say, insignificant creatures?

The visionary poet William Blake also directs our attention to the wonders of nature and cries out passionately against those who misuse animals:

from : Auguries of Innocence

To see a World in a Grain of Sand,
And a Heaven in a Wild Flower,
Hold Infinity in the palm of your hand,
And Eternity in an hour.

A Robin Redbreast in a Cage
Puts all Heaven in a Rage.

A dove-house fill'd with doves and Pigeons
Shudders Hell thro' all its regions.
A dog starv'd at his Master's Gate
Predicts the ruin of the State.

A Horse misused upon the Road
Calls to Heaven for Human blood.
Each outcry of the hunted Hare
A fibre from the Brain does tear.

A Skylark wounded in the wing,
A Cherubim does cease to sing.

William Blake

Activity 4

- What do you think Blake might mean by the first four lines?

Echo

'Who called?' I said, and the words
  Through the whispering glades,
Hither and thither, baffled the birds –
  'Who called? Who called?'

The leafy boughs on high
  Hissed in the sun;
The dark air carried my cry
  Faintingly on:

Eyes in the green, in the shade,
  In the motionless brake,
Voices that said what I said,
  For mockery's sake:

'Who cares?' I bawled through my tears;
  The wind fell low:
In the silence, 'Who cares? Who cares?'
  Wailed to and fro.

Walter de la Mare

Activity 5

- Read the poem *Echo*.
- What seem to you to be the main feelings in the poem?
- Is the 'I' of the poem a child or a grown-up? What are the reasons for your answer?

One way to focus on pictures of feelings is to try **list poems**.
The poet Adrian Henri, remembering his art student days, begins his poem *Love is…* like this:

Love is…

Love is feeling cold in the back of vans
Love is a fanclub with only two fans
Love is walking holding paintstained hands
Love is

Each verse of the poem then follows the same pattern.

Activity 6

- Take one feeling you have fairly often – perhaps excitement, boredom or fear – and simply list five or six experiences or scenes you associate with it. Like Adrian Henri begin your list with 'X is…' and write down each idea on a separate line.

Mixed feelings

Sometimes our feelings are complicated. We may have 'mixed feelings'. The writer of the next poem remembers how he felt when, as a ten-year-old at boarding school his headmaster called him in to give him some news.

The Lesson

'Your father's gone,' my bald headmaster said.
His shiny dome and brown tobacco jar
Splintered at once in tears. It wasn't grief.
I cried for knowledge which was bitterer
Than any grief. For there and then I knew
That grief has uses — that a father dead
Could bind the bully's fist a week or two;
And then I cried for shame, then for relief.

I was a month past ten when I learnt this:
I still remember how the noise was stilled
In school-assembly when my grief came in.
Some goldfish in a bowl quietly sculled
Around their shining prison on its shelf.
They were indifferent. All the other eyes
Were turned towards me. Somewhere in myself
Pride, like a goldfish, flashed a sudden fin.

Edward Lucie-Smith

Activity 7

- Read the poem.
- What conflicting feelings does the boy have when he hears of his father's death? Why?
- What conflicting feelings does he have when his father's death is announced in assembly? Why?

Kate Clanchy remembers her schooldays when she had mixed feelings about Games.

Teams

I would have skipped the stupid games,
long afternoons spent chilled in goal,
or sleepy, scratching, in deep field,
leapt the sagging fence
and learnt, as others do, apparently,
from dying mice, cow parsley,

if it weren't for this persistent sense
of something – like the words to songs,
sung out on the bus
to matches, like my name on lists
on notice boards, shortened
called across the pitch,

trusted by the ones who knew,
the ones with casual shoulders, cool –
that thing, I mean, that knack, that ease,
still sailing, like those hockey balls,
like sodden summer tennis balls,
right past me.

Kate Clanchy

Activity 8

- Why did the writer dislike team games at school?
- What did the others who felt like her do in games lessons?
- What kept her playing?
- What, above all, did she want to be like?
- What suggests that even now, as a grown-up, she feels she didn't quite achieve it?

In the wars

This poem, by Thomas Hardy, is written from the point of view of a soldier thinking about a man he has killed in battle. As he tries to make sense of what he has done, and imagines how things would have turned out if they had met by chance in a pub rather than in battle, we see that he has very mixed feelings about what has happened.

The Man He Killed

Had he and I but met
By some old ancient inn,
We should have set us down to wet
Right many a nipperkin! *   *to drink a good few half-pints of ale

But ranged as infantry, *   *drawn up in opposing lines as foot soldiers
And staring face to face,
I shot at him as he at me,
And killed him in his place.

I shot him dead because—
Because he was my foe *,   *enemy
Just so: my foe of course he was;
That's clear enough; although

He thought he'd 'list *, perhaps,   *short for 'enlist': become a soldier
Off-hand * like—just as I—   *without thinking about it too much
Was out of work—had sold his traps *—   *belongings/tools of his trade
No other reason why.

Yes; quaint and curious * war is!   *odd and strange
You shoot a fellow down
You'd treat *, if met where any bar is,   *buy a drink for
Or help to half a crown. *   *lend two shillings and sixpence (12.5 p) to

Thomas Hardy

Activity 9

- Listen to the poem *The Man He Killed* being read aloud.

- What made the two men enemies?

- What reason does the soldier give for shooting? Is he convinced by this? What suggests he is thinking it over?

- What similarities between the two men are suggested in verse 4?

- What is the tone of the poem? What is the effect of the colloquial (everyday) language the speaker uses?

- What does the soldier think about war?

The Veteran
May, 1916

We came upon him sitting in the sun,
  Blinded by war, and left. And past the fence
There came young soldiers from The Hand and Flower,
  Asking advice of his experience.

And he said this, and that, and told them tales,
  And all the nightmares of each empty head
Blew into air; then hearing us beside,
  'Poor chaps, how'd they know what it's like?' he said.

And we stood there, and watched him as he sat,
  Turning his sockets where they went away,
Until it came to one of us to ask
  'And you're – how old?'
    'Nineteen, the third of May.'

Margaret Postgate Cole

Activity 10

- In Britain, the word 'veteran', when used about a soldier, means
  "Someone who has had long experience in military service; an old
  soldier." Why does the writer choose this word for her title? What
  expectations does it set up and how does the last line make it ironic?

The Send-Off

Down the close, darkening lanes they sang their way
To the siding-shed,
And lined the train with faces grimly gay.

Their breasts were stuck all white with wreath and spray
As men's are, dead.

Dull porters watched them, and a casual tramp
Stood staring hard,
Sorry to miss them from the upland camp.

Then, unmoved, signals nodded, and a lamp
Winked to the guard.

So secretly, like wrongs hushed-up, they went.
They were not ours:
We never heard to which front these were sent;

Nor there if they yet mock what women meant
Who gave them flowers.

Shall they return to beatings of great bells
In wild train-loads?
A few, a few, too few for drums and yells,

May creep back, silent, to village wells,
Up half-known roads.

Wilfred Owen

Activity 11

- Read the poem *The Send-Off*.

- A train-load of soldiers marches to the station to be sent to the battle-front; although they sing, what images suggest they will not return alive?

- What images suggest there is something secretive in their being sent to the battle-front?

- When the survivors return, how will they be welcomed? Why do you think this is? Are there modern parallels?

Owen's poem *Dulce et Decorum Est* takes its title from an inscription often found on war memorials commemorating the dead of the First World War: 'Dulce et Decorum Est Pro Patria Mori'. It means 'It is sweet and fitting to die for one's country.' The reality, as Owen makes all too clear in his description of a chlorine gas attack, may be very different.

Dulce et Decorum Est

Bent double, like old beggars under sacks,
Knock-kneed, coughing like hags, we cursed through sludge,
Till on the haunting flares we turned our backs
And towards our distant rest began to trudge.
Men marched asleep. Many had lost their boots
But limped on, blood-shod. All went lame; all blind;
Drunk with fatigue; deaf even to the hoots
Of tired, outstripped Five-Nines that dropped behind.

Gas! Gas! Quick, boys! – An ecstasy of fumbling,
Fitting the clumsy helmets just in time;
But someone still was yelling out and stumbling
And flound'ring like a man in fire or lime...
Dim, through the misty panes and thick green light,
As under a green sea, I saw him drowning.

In all my dreams, before my helpless sight,
He plunges at me, guttering, choking, drowning.

If in some smothering dreams you too could pace
Behind the wagon that we flung him in,
And watch the white eyes writhing in his face,
His hanging face, like a devil's sick of sin;
If you could hear, at every jolt, the blood
Come gargling from the froth-corrupted lungs,
Obscene as cancer, bitter as the cud
Of vile, incurable sores on innocent tongues,–
My friend, you would not tell with such high zest
To children ardent for some desperate glory,
The old Lie: Dulce et decorum est
Pro patria mori.

Wilfred Owen

Reflection

The mixed feelings in the next poem, *Lost*, come from the writer musing gently about his friend who has a Scottish Catholic father and a Pakistani Muslim mother.

Lost

To quote my distant friend Imran Macleod
'A man with culture has no identity.'

The last I heard from him was, he was off
To the Himalayas.

He had a very confused childhood.

Father was Scottish.
Mother Pakistani.

They'd always be arguing over many things concerning him.

One was religion.

Father wanted him brought up
A Catholic; mother wanted a Muslim.

Was the only boy on our street who went
To mosque on Fridays and chapel on Sundays.

But in the mountains

God's sure to find him.

Hamid Shami

PART TEN THEMES B

Unit 1

SEASONS

Spring

Ted Hughes and e. e. cummings create the sense of spring in quite different ways.

From: Spring Nature Notes

1

The sun lies mild and still on the yard
    stones.

The clue is a solitary daffodil – the first.

And the whole air struggling in soft
    excitements
Like a woman hurrying into her silks.
Birds everywhere zipping and unzipping
Changing their minds, in soft excitements,
Warming their wings and trying their
    voices.

The trees still spindle bare.

Beyond them, from the warmed blue hills
An exhilaration swirls upward, like a huge
    fish.

As under a waterfall, in the bustling pool.

Over the whole land
Spring thunders down in brilliant silence.

5

Spring bulges the hills.
The bare trees creak and shift.
Some buds have burst in tatters –
Like firework stubs.

But winter's lean bullocks
Only pretend to eat
The grass that will not come.

Then they bound like lambs, they twist in
    the air
They bounce their half tons of elastic
When the bale of hay breaks open.

They gambol from heap to heap,
Finally stand happy chewing their beards
Of last summer's dusty whiskers.

6

With arms swinging, a tremendous skater
On the flimsy ice of space,
The earth leans into its curve –

Thrilled to the core, some flies have waded
    out
An inch onto my window, to stand on the
    sky
And try their buzz.

Ted Hughes

Activity 1

- Read the three extracts on page 82.

- Focus on section 1, lines 3–7. On a copy of the poem, using different colours, underline the similes, repetitions and active verbs that Hughes uses to describe the coming of spring.

- Focus on section 5. On a copy of the poem, underline the comparisons Hughes uses to describe the buds on the trees and the bullocks in the fields.

- Talk about the pictures you get in your mind's eye from these descriptions.

In Just-Spring

in Just—
spring   when the world is mud—
luscious the little
lame balloonman

whistles   far   and wee

and eddieandbill come
running from marbles and
piracies and it's
spring

when the world is puddle-wonderful

the queer
old balloonman whistles
far   and   wee
and bettyandisabel come dancing

from hop-scotch and jump-rope and

it's
spring
and
    the

                              goat-footed

balloonMan whistles
far
and
wee

E. E. Cummings

Activity 2

- Read the poem above.

- How does E.E.Cummings play with words and layout to suggest the feeling of spring?

Summer

Ted Hughes creates two contrasting images of summer in his poem, *Work and Play*.

Work and Play

The swallow of summer, she toils all summer,
A blue-dark knot of glittering voltage,
A whiplash swimmer, a fish of the air.
      But the serpent of cars that crawls through the dust
      In shimmering exhaust
      Searching to slake
      Its fever in ocean
      Will play and be idle or else it will bust.

The swallow of summer, the barbed harpoon,
She flings from the furnace, a rainbow of purples,
Dips her glow in the pond and is perfect.
      But the serpent of cars that collapsed at the beach
      Disgorges its organs
      A scamper of colours
      Which roll like tomatoes
      Nude as tomatoes
      With sand in their creases
      To cringe in the sparkle of rollers and screech.

The swallow of summer, the seamstress of summer,
She scissors the blue into shapes and she sews it,
She draws a long thread and she knots it at corners.
      But the holiday people
      Are laid out like wounded
      Flat as in ovens
      Roasting and basting
      With faces of torment as space burns them blue
      Their heads are transistors
      Their teeth grit on sand grains
      Their lost kids are squalling
      While man-eating flies
      Jab electric shock needles but what can they do?

They can climb in their cars with raw bodies, raw faces
> And start up the serpent
> And headache it homeward
> A car full of squabbles
> And sobbing and stickiness
> With sand in their crannies
> Inhaling petroleum
> That pours from the foxgloves
> While the evening swallow
The swallow of summer, cartwheeling through crimson,
Touches the honey-slow river and turning
Returns to the hand stretched from under the eaves—
A boomerang of rejoicing shadow.

Ted Hughes

Activity 3

- List the comparisons Ted Hughes uses to describe the 'swallow of summer'. What pictures of this season do they help to create?

- Now, do the same for 'the serpent of cars' and 'the holiday people'. What picture do you get of the holiday-makers?

- Why do you think Ted Hughes gives the poem this title?

July

(From *The Shepherd's Calendar*)

... noon burns with its blistering breath
Around, and day dies still as death.
The busy noise of man and brute
Is on a sudden lost and mute;
Even the brook that leaps along
Seems weary of its bubbling song,
And, so soft its waters creep,
Tired silence sinks in sounder sleep.
The very flies forget to hum;
And, save the waggon rocking round,
The landscape sleeps without a sound.
The breeze is stopt, the lazy bough

Hath not a leaf that dances now;
The totter-grass upon the hill,
And spiders' threads, are standing still;
The feathers dropt from moor-hen's wing,
Which to the water's surface cling,
Are steadfast, and as heavy seem
As stones beneath them in the stream;
Hawkweed and groundsel's fanning downs
Unruffled keep their seedy crowns;
And in the oven-heated air,
Not one light thing is floating there,
Save that to the earnest eye,
The restless heat seems twittering by.

John Clare

Autumn

An Autumn Morning

The autumn morning, waked by many a gun,
Throws o'er the fields her many-coloured light,
Wood wildly touched, close tanned, and
 stubbles dun,
A motley paradise for earth's delight;
Clouds ripple as the darkness breaks to light,
And clover plots are hid with silver mist,
One shower of cobwebs o'er the surface
 spread;
And threads of silk in strange disorder twist
Round every leaf and blossom's bottly head;
Hares in the drowning herbage scarcely steal
But on the battered pathway squat abed
And by the cart-rut nip their morning meal.
Look where we may, the scene is strange
 and new,
And every object wears a changing hue.

John Clare

Activity 4

- Pick out two or three details that John Clare suggests are typical of this season. Can you add any of your own?

Leaves

Who's killed the leaves?
         Me, says the apple, I've killed them all.
         Fat as a bomb or a cannonball
         I've killed the leaves.

Who sees them drop?

> Me, says the pear, they will leave me all bare
> So all the people can point and stare.
> I see them drop.

Who'll catch their blood?

> Me, me, me, says the marrow, the marrow.
> I'll get so rotund that they'll need a wheelbarrow.
> I'll catch their blood.

Who'll make their shroud?

> Me, says the swallow, there's just time enough
> Before I must pack all my spools and be off.
> I'll make their shroud.

Who'll dig their grave?

> Me, says the river, with the power of the clouds
> A brown deep grave I'll dig under my floods.
> I'll dig their grave.

Who'll be their parson?

> Me, says the Crow, for it is well-known
> I study the bible right down to the bone.
> I'll be their parson.

Who'll be chief mourner?

> Me, says the wind, I will cry through the grass
> The people will pale and go cold when I pass.
> I'll be chief mourner.

Who'll carry the coffin?

> Me, says the sunset, the whole world will weep
> To see me lower it into the deep.
> I'll carry the coffin.

Who'll sing a psalm?

> Me, says the tractor, with my gear grinding glottle
> I'll plough up the stubble and sing through my throttle.
> I'll sing the psalm.

Who'll toll the bell?

> Me, says the robin, my song in October
> Will tell the still gardens the leaves are over.
> I'll toll the bell.

Ted Hughes

Activity 5

- Do you recognise the pattern of question and answer that goes to make up the story of the poem *Leaves* (there's a clue in the last verse)?

- As a class, read the poem aloud. A good way to do this is to have one person ask all the questions at the start of each verse and then others to read the three-line replies of the apple, the pear, the marrow and so on.

- Each verse is a tiny word-picture, a bit like a haiku. Only here the pictures are put together to tell an autumn story about the death and funeral of the leaves.

- Illustrate the poem either by:

  - Drawing and colouring a series of ten pictures, one for each verse, which can be put up as a wall display, or

  - Designing one large picture, perhaps a poster, which includes each of the things mentioned in the ten verses. Think carefully about the layout. Which figure is the most important? Is it better to make your picture tall and thin to catch the fall of the leaves from the tree to the grave, or to place the objects in a wide landscape?

  Try to include as many of the words of the poem as possible in your illustration.

Winter

Snow in the Suburbs

Every branch big with it,
Bent every twig with it;
Every fork like a white web-foot;
Every street and pavement mute:
Some flakes have lost their way, and grope back upward,
    when
Meeting those meandering down they turn and descend
    again.
The palings are glued together like a wall,
And there is no waft of wind with the fleecy fall.

A sparrow enters the tree,
Whereon immediately
A snow-lump thrice his own slight size
Descends on him and showers his head and eyes.
And overturns him,
And near inurns him,
And lights on a nether twig, when its brush
Starts off a volley of other lodging lumps with a rush.

The steps are a blanched slope,
Up which, with feeble hope,
A black cat comes, wide-eyed and thin;
And we take him in.

Thomas Hardy

Hard Frost

Frost called to water 'Halt!'
And crusted the moist snow with sparkling salt;
Brooks, their own bridges, stop,
And icicles in long stalactites drop,
And tench in water-holes
Lurk under gluey glass like fish in bowls.

In the hard-rutted lane
At every footstep breaks a brittle pane,
And tinkling trees ice-bound,
Changed into weeping willows, sweep the ground;
Dead boughs take root in ponds
And ferns on windows shoot their ghostly fronds.

But vainly the fierce frost
Interns poor fish, ranks trees in an armed host,
Hangs daggers from house-eaves
And on the windows ferny ambush weaves;
In the long war grown warmer
The sun will strike him dead and strip his armour.

Andrew Young

Activity 6

Notice how the three sections of Thomas Hardy's poem move from setting the scene after a heavy snowfall, to the effects of a sparrow perching on a tree, to a cat picking its way up some steps.

Andrew Young's word-picture is full of comparisons to describe the frost, icicles, fish under the ice, frozen puddles, ice-bound trees...

- How is frost portrayed? What military images can you find? Five? Six? More?
- What is the word used when something like frost or summer is described as though they were a person?

But not all seasons are the same as those we experience in Western Europe. The next poem describes the coming of the dry season which alternates with the rainy season on much of Ghana.

The Dry Season

The year is withering; the wind
Blows down the leaves;
Men stand under eaves
And overhear the secrets
Of the cold dry wind,
Of the half-bare trees.

The grasses are tall and tinted
Straw-gold hues of dryness,
And the contradicting awareness,
Of the dusty roads a- scatter
With the pools of colourful leaves,
With ghosts of the dreaming year.

And soon, soon the fires,
The fires will begin to burn
The hawk will flutter and turn
On its wings and swoop for the mouse,
The dogs will run for the hare,
The hare for its little life.

Kwesi Brew

Unit 2

NONSENSE AND STUFF

Many of the poems in this unit are suitable for reading aloud, choral speaking and performing.

Macavity: The Mystery Cat

Macavity's a Mystery Cat: he's called the Hidden Paw—
For he's the master criminal who can defy the Law.
He's the bafflement of Scotland Yard, the Flying Squad's despair:
For when they reach the scene of crime—*Macavity's not there!*

Macavity, Macavity, there's no one like Macavity,
He's broken every human law, he breaks the law of gravity.
His powers of levitation would make a fakir stare,
And when you reach the scene of crime—*Macavity's not there!*
You may seek him in the basement, you may look up in the air—
But I tell you once and once again, *Macavity's not there!*

Macavity's a ginger cat, he's very tall and thin;
You would know him if you saw him, for his eyes are sunken in.
His brow is deeply lined with thought, his head is highly domed;
His coat is dusty from neglect, his whiskers are uncombed.
He sways his head from side to side, with movements like a snake;
And when you think he's half asleep, he's always wide awake.

Macavity, Macavity, there's no one like Macavity,
For he's a fiend in feline shape, a monster of depravity.
You may meet him in a by-street, you may see him in the square—
But when a crime's discovered, then *Macavity's not there!*

He's outwardly respectable. (They say he cheats at cards.)
And his footprints are not found in any file of Scotland Yard's.
And when the larder's looted, or the jewel-case is rifled,
Or when the milk is missing, or another Peke's been stifled,
Or the greenhouse glass is broken, and the trellis past repair—
Ay, there's the wonder of the thing! *Macavity's not there!*

And when the Foreign Office find a Treaty's gone astray,
Or the Admiralty lose some plans and drawings by the way,
There may be a scrap of paper in the hall or on the stair—
But it's useless to investigate—*Macavity's not there!*

And when the loss has been disclosed, the Secret Service say:
'It *must* have been Macavity!'—but he's a mile away.
You'll be sure to find him resting, or a-licking of his thumbs,
Or engaged in doing complicated long division sums.

Macavity, Macavity, there's no one like Macavity,
There never was a Cat of such deceitfulness and suavity,
He always has an alibi, and one or two to spare:
At whatever time the deed took place—MACAVITY WASN'T THERE!
And they say that all the Cats whose wicked deeds are widely known
(I might mention Mungojerrie, I might mention Griddlebone)
Are nothing more than agents for the Cat who all the time
Just controls their operations: the Napoleon of Crime!

T. S. Eliot

Activity 1

The poem describes a cat who reminds us of the master criminal, Moriarty, who was Sherlock Holmes's arch enemy. His exploits are quite remarkable and need to be treated with the amazement they deserve!

• Prepare a reading of the poem with seven people each reading a verse and everybody joining in with 'Macavity's not there!'

The *Hairy Toe* tells the story of an old lady who makes an unusual find in her garden. It is a very old English story but this is the later American version.

The Hairy Toe

Once there was a woman went out to pick
    beans
and she found a Hairy Toe.
She took the Hairy Toe home with her,
and that night, when she went to bed,
the wind began to moan and groan.
Away off in the distance
she seemed to heart a voice crying,
'Where's my Hair-r-ry To-o-oe?
Who's got my Hair-r-ry To-o-oe?'

The woman scrooched down,
'way down under the covers,
and about that time
the wind appeared to hit the house,

smoosh,

and the old house creaked and cracked
like something was trying to get in.
The voice had come nearer,
almost at the door now,
and it said,
'Where's my Hair-r-ry To-o-oe?
Who's got my Hair-r-ry To-o-oe?'

The woman scrooched further down
under the covers
and pulled them tight around her head.

The wind growled around the house
like some big animal
and r-r-um-mbled
over the chimbley.
All at once she heard the door cr-r-a-ack
and Something slipped in
and began to creep over the floor.

The floor went
cre-e-eak, cre-e-eak
at every step that thing took towards her
    bed.
The woman could almost feel
it bending over her bed.
There in an awful voice it said:
'Where's my Hair-r-ry To-o-oe?
Who's got my Hair-r-ry To-o-oe?
YOU'VE GOT IT!'

Anon
(Traditional American)

Activity 2

- Rehearse a reading of the poem with a narrator taking the main part and everybody joining in for the choruses and the last lines. One group can be responsible for sound effects.

In his poem *Alternative Endings to an Unwritten Ballad*, Paul Dehn writes six possible last verses to a poem he in fact never wrote. Most of the six verses end with the ghastly death of his imagined character, Mrs Ravoon. In the sixth verse she gets a new lease of life!

Alternative Endings to an Uwritten Ballad

I stole through the dungeons, while everyone slept,
    Till I came to the cage where the Monster was kept.
There, locked in the arms of a Giant Baboon,
    Rigid and smiling, lay ... MRS RAVOON!

I climbed the clock-tower in the first morning sun
    And 'twas midday at least ere my journey was done;
But the clock never sounded the last stroke of noon,
    For there, from the clapper, swung MRS RAVOON.

I hauled in the line, and I took my first look
    At the half-eaten horror that hung from the hook.
I had dragged from the depths of the limpid lagoon
    The luminous body of MRS RAVOON.

I fled in the tempest, through lightning and thunder,
    And there, as a flash split the darkness asunder,
Chewing a rat's-tail and mumbling a rune,
    Mad in the moat squatted MRS RAVOON.

I stood by the waters so green and so thick,
    And I stirred at the scum with my old, withered stick;
When there rose through the ooze, like a monstrous balloon,
    The bloated cadaver of MRS RAVOON.

Facing the fens, I looked back from the shore
    Where all had been empty a moment before;
And there, by the light of the Lincolnshire moon,
    Immense on the marshes stood ... MRS RAVOON!

Paul Dehn

Activity 3

- Working in groups, read a verse each and see which group can produce the most horrifying rendering of this melodramatic tale.

- Try writing your own Mrs Ravoon verse (tricky as there aren't many other rhyming words left, though you could consider 'spoon', 'boon', 'loon', 'soon', 'croon', 'dune', 'prune', 'tune' and perhaps 'strewn' and 'hewn'). Or write your verses for another character with a different name.

We first came across limericks on page **7**. Limericks, like the ones below have five lines. Lines 1, 2, and 5 of limericks have seven to ten syllables and rhyme with one another making a triplet. Lines 3 and 4 have five to seven syllables and also rhyme with each other as a couplet.

Each night Father fills me with dread
When he sits at the foot of my bead;
    I'd not mind that he speaks
    In gibbers and squeaks,
But for seventeen years he's been dead.

Edward Gorey

There was an old person of Stroud,
Who was horribly jammed in a crowd;
    Some she slew with a kick, some she
        scrunched with a stick,
That impulsive old person of Stroud.

Edward Lear

There was a young lady called Wemyss
Who, it semyss was troubled with dremyss.
    She would wake in the night
    And, in terrible fright,
Shake the bemyss of the house with her scremyss.

Anon

There was an old fellow of Tring
Who, when somebody asked him to sing,
    Replied, 'Ain't it odd?
    I can never tell *God*
Save the Weasel from *Pop goes the King*.'

Anon

Activity 4

- Write your own limerick. It isn't difficult as long as you remember that:

  - Limericks usually begin with a line that mentions the subject such as 'A teacher of maths at our school';

  - They rhyme in the way shown above;

  - The last line is often, though not always, a 'punch line' and contains a joke. Edward Lear, who wrote many limericks, often did not end his with joke lines. He simply repeated the idea from the first line, e.g. 'That crazy old fellow from Ryde'.

Ruthless Rhymes is the title Harry Graham gave to his four-line verses like *Appreciation* and *The Stern Parent*. They have two pairs of rhyming lines (couplets) and have to be very unkind, hence *Ruthless Rhymes*.

Appreciation

Auntie did you feel no pain
Falling from that willow tree?
Will you do it, please, again?
Cos my friend here didn't see.

Harry Graham

The Stern Parent

Father heard his Children scream,
So he threw them in the stream,
Saying, as he drowned the third,
'Children should be seen, not heard!'

Harry Graham

Activity 5

- Compose your own Ruthless Rhyme and draw a picture to go with it.

Ye Tortures is complete nonsense, but the pictures suggested by the words have a kind of idiotic sense that makes people laugh.

Ye Tortures

From the document found in the Archives of Bude Monastery during a squirting excavation. It shows a complete list of tortures approved by the Ministry of Works in the year 1438, for failure to pay leg tithe, or sockage.

The prisoner will be:

Bluned on ye Grunions
   and krelled on his Grotts
Ye legges will be twergled
   and pulled thru' ye motts!

His Nukes will be Fongled
   split thrice on yon Thulls
Then laid on ye Quottle
   and hung by ye Bhuls!

Twice thocked on the Phneffic,
   Yea broggled thrice twee.
Ye moggs will be grendled
   and stretched six foot three!

By now, if ye victim
   show not ye sorrow,
Send him home. Tell him,
   'Come back to-morrow.'

Spike Milligan

97

Activity 6

- Try to write an additional verse with tortures Spike Milligan might have included.

Unit 3

MAGIC AND MYSTERY

You can, of course, simply read and enjoy each of these poems individually, but another way of approaching them is as performance poems, where you can have different groups or individuals working on a poem each and then presenting their readings as a sequence.

The Magic Wood

The wood is full of shining eyes,
The wood is full of creeping feet,
The wood is full of tiny cries:
You must not go to the wood at night!

I met a man with eyes of glass
And a finger as curled as the wriggling
    worm,
And hair all red with rotting leaves,
And a stick that hissed like a summer snake.

The wood is full of shining eyes,
The wood is full of creeping feet,
The wood is full of tiny cries:
You must not go to the wood at night!

He sang me a song in backwards words,
And drew me a dragon in the air.
I saw his teeth through the back of his head,
And a rat's eyes winking from his hair.

The wood is full of shining eyes,
The wood is full of creeping feet,
The wood is full of tiny cries:
You must not go to the wood at night!

He made me a penny out of a stone,
And showed me the way to catch a lark
With a straw and a nut and a whispered
    word
And a pennorth of ginger wrapped up in a
    leaf.

The wood is full of shining eyes,
The wood is full of creeping feet,
The wood is full of tiny cries:
You must not go to the wood at night!

He asked me my name, and where I lived:
I told him a name from my Book of Tales;
He asked me to come with him into the
    wood
And dance with the Kings from under the
    hills.

The wood is full of shining eyes,
The wood is full of creeping feet,
The wood is full of tiny cries:
You must not go to the wood at night!

But I saw that his eyes were turning to fire;
I watched the nails grow on his wriggling
    hand;
And I said my prayers, all out in a rush,
And found myself safe on my father's land.

Oh, the wood is full of shining eyes,
The wood is full of creeping feet,
The wood is full of tiny cries:
You must not go to the wood at night!

Henry Treece

Activity 1

- *The Magic Wood* can make a powerful performance. As a group, decide the best way to perform the poem. The main story can be read by just one voice or shared between five voices. The hypnotic, chanted chorus can be said by a large group or by different smaller groups.

Hist whist

hist   whist
little ghostthings
tip-toe
twinkle-toe

little twitchy
witches and tingling
goblins
hob-a-nob   hob-a-nob

little hoppy happy
toad in tweeds
tweeds
little itchy mousies

with scuttling
eyes   rustle and run   and
hidehidehide
whisk

whisk   look out for the old woman
with the wart on her nose
what she'll do to yer
nobody knows

for she knows the devil   ooch
the devil   ouch
the devil
ach   the great

green
dancing
devil
devil

devil
devil

wheeEEE

e. e. cummings

Activity 2

- In groups of three, perform the poem. Try alternating solo, duet and trio parts to create light, quick, witchy sounds.

The Listeners, by Walter de la Mare, has delighted and puzzled readers since it was first published. It contains many of the themes found in his poetry including death, dreams and mystery all tinged with a feeling of sadness.

The Listeners

'Is there anybody there?' said the Traveller,
  Knocking on the moonlit door;
And his horse in the silence champed the grasses
  Of the forest's ferny floor:
And a bird flew up out of the turret,
  Above the Traveller's head:
And he smote upon the door again a second time;
  'Is there anybody there?' he said.
But no one descended to the Traveller;
  No head from the leaf-fringed sill
Leaned over and looked into his grey eyes,
  Where he stood perplexed and still.
But only a host of phantom listeners
  That dwelt in the lone house then
Stood listening in the quiet of the moonlight
  To that voice from the world of men:
Stood thronging the faint moonbeams on the dark stair,
  That goes down to the empty hall,

Hearkening in an air stirred and shaken
  By the lonely Traveller's call.
And he felt in his heart their strangeness,
  Their stillness answering his cry,
While his horse moved, cropping the dark turf,
  'Neath the starred and leafy sky;
For he suddenly smote on the door, even
  Louder, and lifted his head: –
'Tell them I came, and no one answered,
  That I kept my word,' he said.
Never the least stir made the listeners,
  Though every word he spake
Fell echoing through the shadowiness of the still house
  From the one man left awake:
Ay, they heard his foot upon the stirrup,
  And the sound of iron on stone,
And how the silence surged softly backward,
  When the plunging hoofs were gone.

Walter de la Mare

Activity 3

- Read the poem and, with a friend, discuss what you think it is about.
- In small groups, prepare readings of the poem, splitting the words between different voices.

Another poem by Walter de la Mare, *The Ghost*, has similar ideas to *The Listeners*. It is a conversation between two voices – one that of a living person and the other that of a ghost.

The Ghost

'Who knocks?' 'I, who was beautiful,
  Beyond all dreams to restore,
I, from the roots of the dark thorn am hither,
  And knock on the door.'

'Who speaks?' 'I – once was my speech
  Sweet as the bird's on the air,
When echo lurks by the waters to heed;
  'Tis I speak thee fair.'

'Dark is the hour?' 'Ay, and cold.'
  'Lone is my house.' 'Ah, but mine?'
'Sight, touch, lips, eyes yearned in vain.'
  'Long dead these to thine...'

Silence. Still faint on the porch
  Brake the flames of the stars.
In gloom groped a hope-wearied hand
  Over keys, bolts, and bars.

A face peered. All the grey night
  In chaos of vacancy shone;
Nought but vast sorrow was there –
  The sweet cheat gone.

Walter de la Mare

Activity 4

- Read the poem.
- Discuss what you think is happening and what the relationship between the two voices is or might have been.
- In pairs, prepare a reading of the poem.

Charles Causley's poem *Tell Me, Tell Me, Sarah Jane* is a twentieth-century ballad. Like many of Causley's poems it draws on much older traditional Cornish stories of magic and here, possibly of mermaids and the lure of the sea.

Tell Me, Tell Me, Sarah Jane

Tell me, tell me, Sarah Jane,
    Tell me, dearest daughter,
Why are you holding in your hand
    A thimbleful of water?
Why do you hold it to your eye
    And gaze both late and soon
From early morning light until
    The rising of the moon?

Mother, I hear the mermaids cry,
    I hear the mermen sing,
And I can see the sailing ships
    All made of sticks and string.
And I can see the jumping fish,
    The whales that fall and rise
And swim about the waterspout,
    That swarms up to the skies.

Tell me, tell me, Sarah Jane,
    Tell your darling mother,
Why do you walk beside the tide
    As though you loved none other?
Why do you listen to a shell
    And watch the billows curl,
And throw away your diamond ring
    And wear instead the pearl?

Mother, I hear the water
    Beneath the headland pinned,
And I can see the seagull
    Sliding down the wind.
I taste the salt upon my tongue
    As sweet as sweet can be.

Tell me, my dear, whose voice you hear?

It is the sea, the sea.

                            Charles Causley

Activity 5

- Prepare a reading of the poem with one voice taking the part of the mother and the other one that of the daughter.

Another, more ghostly, story by Charles Causley is the one he tells in his poem *Miller's End*.

Miller's End

When we moved to Miller's End,
    Every afternoon at four
A thin shadow of a shade
    Quavered through the garden-door.

Dressed in black from top to toe
    And a veil about her head
To us all it seemed as though
    She came walking from the dead.

With a basket on her arm
    Through the hedge-gap she would
        pass
Never a mark that we could spy
    On the flagstones or the grass.

When we told the garden-boy
    How we saw the phantom glide,
With a grin his face was bright
    As the pool he stood beside.

'That's no ghost-walk,' Billy said,
    'Nor a ghost you fear to stop –
Only old Mrs Wickerby.
    On a short cut to the shop.'

So next day we lay in wait,
    Passed a civil time of day
Said how pleased we were she came
    Daily down our garden way.

Suddenly her cheek it paled,
    Turned, as quick, from ice to flame.
'Tell me,' said Mrs Wickerby.
    'Who spoke of me, and my name?'

'Bill the garden-boy.'
    She sighed,
Said, of course, you could not know
    How he drowned – that very pool –
A frozen winter – long ago.'

Charles Causley

Activity 6

- Read the poem. Make sure you understand the twist at the end.

- In threes, prepare your own reading of the poem with voices for the narrator, Billy and Mrs Wickerby.

The story of how the next poem came to be written is well-known. The poet fell asleep while reading about the Khan (a prince or ruler) Kubla and the palace he had commanded to be built. When he woke up he was aware that he had composed two or three hundred lines on this theme in his head and he quickly began to write them down. Unfortunately, he was then interrupted by 'a person from Porlock', a nearby village. When he returned to his task he had forgotten all but this fragment of 54 lines.

Kubla Khan

In Xanadu did Kubla Khan
A stately pleasure-dome decree:
Where Alph, the sacred river, ran
Through caverns measureless to man
Down to a sunless sea.
So twice five miles of fertile ground
With walls and towers were girdled round:
And there were gardens bright with sinuous rills,
Where blossomed many an incense-bearing tree;
And here were forests ancient as the hills,
Enfolding sunny spots of greenery.
But oh! that deep romantic chasm which slanted
Down the green hill athwart a cedarn cover!
A savage place! as holy and enchanted
As e'er beneath a waning moon was haunted
By woman wailing for her demon-lover!
And from this chasm, with ceaseless turmoil seething,
As if this earth in fast thick pants were breathing,
A mighty fountain momently was forced:
Amid whose swift half-intermitted burst
Huge fragments vaulted like rebounding hail,
Or chaffy grain beneath the thresher's flail:
And 'mid these dancing rocks at once and ever
It flung up momently the sacred river.
Five miles meandering with a mazy motion
Through wood and dale the sacred river ran,
Then reached the caverns measureless to man,
And sank in tumult to a lifeless ocean:
And 'mid this tumult Kubla heard from far
Ancestral voices prophesying war!

The shadow of the dome of pleasure
Floated midway on the waves;
Where was heard the mingled measure
From the fountain and the caves.
It was a miracle of rare device,
A sunny pleasure-dome with caves of ice!

A damsel with a dulcimer
In a vision once I saw:
It was an Abyssinian maid,
And on her dulcimer she played,
Singing of Mount Abora.
Could I revive within me
Her symphony and song,
To such a deep delight 'twould win me,
That with music loud and long,
I would build that dome in air,
That sunny dome! Those caves of ice!
And all who heard should see them there,
And all should cry, Beware! Beware!
His flashing eyes, his floating hair!
Weave a circle round him thrice,
And close your eyes with holy dread,
For he on honey-dew hath fed,
And drunk the milk of Paradise.

Samuel Taylor Coleridge

Activity 7

- Read the poem. It falls into two parts: the first 36 lines describe an enclosed park with the palace or 'stately pleasure dome' at its centre; the remaining lines, beginning 'A damsel with a dulcimer', give another vision where the poet claims he can build a finer, more magical dome than Kubla's.

- Find the lines in the poem that describe the following details of the dream and talk about the pictures they present in your mind's eye:

continued

Activity 7 – continued

- *the subterranean river Alph* which bursts from a chasm in a 'mighty fountain', the caverns on its course and the 'sunless sea' into which it flows;

- *the landscape* around this sacred river with its walled gardens and ancient forests;

- *the dome itself* rising above this artificial paradise, ten miles in diameter, which casts its shadow on the water.

- Now, draw a map of the area, perhaps with small inset pictures of the main details and phrases from the poem as captions.

Unit 4
STORIES

The History of the Flood

Bang Bang Bang
Said the nails in the Ark.

It's getting rather dark
Said the nails in the Ark.

For the rain is coming down
Said the nails in the Ark.

And you're all like to drown
Said the nails in the Ark.

Dark and black as sin
Said the nails in the Ark.

So won't you all come in
Said the nails in the Ark.

But only two by two
Said the nails in the Ark.

So they came in two by two,
The elephant, the kangaroo,
And the gnu,
And the little tiny shrew.

Then the birds
Flocked in like winged words:
Two racket-tailed motmots, two macaws,
Two nuthatches and two
Little bright robins.

And the reptiles: the gila monster, the slow-
    worm,
The green mamba, the cottonmouth and the
    alligator–
All squirmed in;
And after a very lengthy walk,
Two giant Galapagos tortoises.

And the insects in their hierarchies:
A queen ant, a king ant, a queen wasp, a
    king wasp,
A queen bee, a king bee,
And all the beetles, bugs and mosquitoes,
Cascaded in like glittering, murmurous
    jewels.

But the fish had their wish;
For the rain came down.
People began to drown:
The wicked, the rich–
They gasped out bubbles of pure gold,
Which exhalations
Rose to the constellations.

So for forty days and forty nights
They were on the waste of waters
In those cramped quarters.
It was very dark, damp and lonely.
There was nothing to see, but only
The rain which continued to drop.
It did not stop.

So Noah sent forth a Raven.
The raven said 'Kark!
I will not go back to the Ark.'
The raven was footloose,
He fed on the bodies of the rich–
Rich with vitamins and goo.
They had become bloated,
And everywhere they floated.

The raven's heart was black,
He did not come back.

It was not a nice thing to do:
Which is why the raven is a token of wrath,
And creaks like a rusty gate
When he crosses your path; and Fate
Will grant you no luck that day:
The raven is fey:
You were meant to have a scare.
Fortunately in England
The raven is rather rare.

Then Noah sent forth a dove
She did not want to rove.
She longed for her love—
The other turtle dove—
(For her no other dove!)
She brought back a twig from an olive-tree.
There is no more beautiful tree
Anywhere on the earth,
Even when it comes to birth
From six weeks under the sea.

She did not want to rove.
She wanted to take her rest,
And to build herself a nest
All in the olive grove.
She wanted to make love.
She thought that was the best—

The dove was not a rover;
So they knew that the rain was over.
Noah and his wife got out
(They had become rather stout)
And Japhet, Ham and Shem.
(The same could be said of them.)
They looked up at the sky.
The earth was becoming dry.

Then the animals came ashore—
There were more of them than before:
There were two dogs and a litter of puppies;
There were a tom-cat and two tib-cats
And two litters of kittens—cats
Do not obey regulations;
And, as you might expect,
A quantity of rabbits.

God put a rainbow in the sky.
They wondered what it was for.
There had never been a rainbow before.
The rainbow was a sign;
It looked like a neon sign—
Seven colours arched in the skies:
What should it publicize?
They looked up with wondering eyes.

It advertises Mercy
Said the nails in the Ark.

Mercy Mercy Mercy
Said the nails in the Ark.

Our God is merciful
Said the nails in the Ark.

Merciful and gracious
Bang Bang Bang Bang.

John Heath-Stubbs

Activity 1

- The poem can be performed or recorded. The nails in the Ark are heard at the beginning and end of the poem and you might have sound effects of hammering behind the first seven sections and last four sections of the poem.

- The reading of the sections can be shared out in various ways but you might experiment with choral speaking for the nails and, in between, different voices for the sections on the birds, the reptiles, the insects, the fish, the raven, the dove, the coming ashore and the rainbow.

The poem of *The Rime of the Ancient Mariner* is set in the time of the sailing ships when the wind was the only source of power. It is a horror story told by the sole survivor of a fateful voyage.

The poem is so visual it is almost like a horror film, as you will see in the extract below. Part 1 of the poem describes the ship's voyage south into the Polar seas and ends when the Mariner shoots an albatross, the sailors' bird of good fortune, which had been following them. Part 2 describes the ship idle in the ocean without wind for many days: 'As idle as a painted ship/ upon a painted ocean'. The crew, starving without food or water, blame the Mariner for their plight and hang the dead albatross around his neck in place of his cross. This extract, Part 3, continues the story as hopes rise when the Mariner sees a ship sailing towards them, mysteriously moving without wind or tide.

The full poem can be found on the *Touchstones Now Dynamic Learning Network CD-ROM*.

Excerpt from The Rime of the Ancient Mariner

PART III

'There passed a weary time. Each throat
Was parched, and glazed each eye.
A weary time! a weary time!
How glazed each weary eye,
When looking westward, I beheld
A something in the sky.

At first it seemed a little speck,
And then it seemed a mist;
It moved and moved, and took at last
A certain shape, I wist.

A speck, a mist, a shape, I wist!
And still it neared and neared:
As if it dodged a water-sprite,
It plunged and tacked and veered.

With throats unslaked, with black lips
  baked,
We could nor laugh nor wail;
Through utter drought all dumb we stood!
I bit my arm, I sucked the blood,
And cried, A sail! a sail!

With throats unslaked, with black lips
  baked,
Agape they heard me call:
Gramercy! they for joy did grin,
And all at once their breath drew in,
As they were drinking all.

See! see! (I cried) she tacks no more!
Hither to work us weal;
Without a breeze, without a tide,
She steadies with upright keel!

The western wave was all a-flame.
The day was well nigh done!
Almost upon the western wave
Rested the broad bright Sun;
When that strange shape drove suddenly
Betwixt us and the Sun.

And straight the Sun was flecked with bars,
(Heaven's Mother send us grace!)
As if through a dungeon-grate he peered
With broad and burning face.

Alas! (thought I, and my heart beat loud)
How fast she nears and nears!
Are those her sails that glance in the Sun,
Like restless gossameres?

Are those her ribs through which the Sun
Did peer, as through a grate?
And is that Woman all her crew?
Is that a Death? and are there two?
Is Death that woman's mate?

Her lips were red, her looks were free,
Her locks were yellow as gold:
Her skin was as white as leprosy,
The Nightmare Life-in-Death was she,
Who thicks man's blood with cold.

The naked hulk alongside came,
And the twain were casting dice:
"The game is done! I've won! I've won."
Quoth she, and whistles thrice.

The Sun's rim dips; the stars rush out:
At one stride comes the dark;
With far-heard whisper, o'er the sea,
Off shot the spectre-bark.

We listened and looked sideways up!
Fear at my heart, as at a cup,
My life-blood seemed to sip!
The stars were dim, and thick the night,
The steersman's face by his lamp gleamed
  white;

From the sails the dew did drip–
Till clomb above the eastern bar
The horned Moon, with one bright star
Within the nether tip.

One after one, by the star-dogged Moon,
Too quick for groan or sigh,
Each turned his face with a ghastly pang,
And cursed me with his eye.

Four times fifty living men,
(And I heard nor sigh nor groan)
With heavy thump, a lifeless lump,
They dropped down one by one.

The souls did from their bodies fly,–
They fled to bliss or woe!
And every soul, it passed me by,
Like the whizz of my cross-bow!'

Samuel Taylor Coleridge

The next poem tells of the age-old custom of smuggling goods across the English Channel to the isolated villages of Devon and Cornwall, which was very common in years gone by. The smugglers were known in their villages and were often well-regarded even by the local clergy. The Excise men – the King's officers – were seen as interfering with a long established trade. The local inhabitants did not see why they should pay the king in far-off London excise duty or tax on the goods they brought ashore. The smugglers were called the Gentlemen, and if you were a child, it was best you did not know who they were or what they were up to. After all, a convicted smuggler could be condemned to death.

A Smuggler's Song

If you wake at midnight, and hear a horse's feet,
Don't go drawing back the blind, or looking in the street.
Them that asks no questions isn't told a lie.
Watch the wall, my darling, while the Gentlemen go by!
     Five and twenty ponies,
     Trotting through the dark –
     Brandy for the Parson,
     'Baccy for the Clerk;
Laces for a lady, letters for a spy,
And watch the wall, my darling, while the Gentlemen go by!

Running round the woodlump if you chance to find
Little barrels, roped and tarred, all full of brandy-wine,
Don't you shout to come and look, nor use 'em for your play.
Put the brushwood back again, – and they'll be gone next day!

If you see the stable-door setting open wide;
If you see a tired horse lying down inside;
If your mother mends a coat cut about and tore;
If the lining's wet and warm – don't you ask no more!

If you meet King George's men, dressed in blue and red,
You be careful what you say, and mindful what is said.
If they call you 'pretty maid', and chuck you 'neath the chin,
Don't you tell where no one is, nor yet where no one's been!

Knocks and footsteps round the house – whistles after dark –
You've no call for running out till the house-dogs bark.
Trusty's here, and *Pincher's* here, and see how dumb they lie –
They don't fret to follow when the Gentlemen go by!

If you do as you've been told, 'likely there's a chance
You'll be give a dainty doll, all the way from France,
With a cap of Valenciennes, and a velvet hood –
A present from the Gentlemen, along o' being good!
      Five and twenty ponies,
      Trotting through the dark –
      Brandy for the Parson,
      'Baccy for the Clerk;
Them that asks no questions isn't told a lie –
Watch the wall, my darling, while the Gentlemen go by!

Rudyard Kipling

Activity 2

- Prepare a reading of the poem *A Smuggler's Song*. You could choose to have a smuggler father or mother speaking to a daughter. Alternatively, you could have a number of different smugglers' voices reading the different warning sentences and a chorus of voices reading the two repeated sections that begin 'Five and twenty ponies'. Try to maintain the steady rhythm that reminds us of the ponies' hooves throughout the poem.

The story about *James* in the next poem was written for a young relative as a modern version of Hilaire Belloc's *Cautionary Verses*.

James

Who played computer games but finally got a life

The chief delight of youthful James
Was violent computer games,
Where everything was quite destroyed.
But most of all the lad enjoyed
The buxom charms of Lara Croft,
Despite the fact his sister scoffed
And called him 'weird, a total nerd',
And found his passion quite absurd,
And said he ought to 'get a life'—
Thus causing much familial strife.

(This Lara, if you didn't know,
Creation of the Eidos Co.,
Is no bloodless Space Invader
But heroine of their game Tomb Raider,
Quick-thinking, weapon-toting, strong
—With legs so very, very long...)

But we digress from young James' plight.
He'd stay up playing every night
Until his eyes were raw and red;
For years he hardly went to bed.
He couldn't leave the thing alone
And wore his fingers to the bone
Tapping the keyboard fev'rishly
Trying to get from level three
To four — or was it five to six?
No matter — he'd got to have his fix.

His parents, in complete despair,
Pleaded with him, tore their hair,
Called in a psychiatrist
Who warned the boy he should desist
And go for healthy walks and ride
His bicycle, not lurk inside,
Confined entirely to his room
Whose matt black walls and general gloom
Lit only by his screen display,
Depressed the spirit, were not gay.

Young James grew older, tall and wan,
His energy was almost gone
When (happy chance!) he glanced outside
And saw, a vision slowly glide
Along the sidewalk on her bike,
Laughing and waving, quite unlike
Lara or girls he'd seen before.
A girl called Jill had moved next door.
Immediately, his heart went bump,
Against his ribs he felt it thump.

The rest you know, or you can guess.
No longer now a total mess
In thrall to his computer screen,
James has a real, not virtual, queen.

His old computer gathers dust
And Lara's blasters, legs and bust
Are all forgotten now you see:
And James is just like you and me.
But every day he thanks the fates
That made him happy with Jill Gates!

Peter Benton

Activity 3

- Read the poem *James*. Do you know anyone obsessed with something as James was with computers? What sorts of things?

- Think of another modern habit that maybe needs a warning and write your own cautionary verse about it. Perhaps walking down a crowded street or driving when using a mobile, listening to an iPod in class etc.

The Lion and Albert

There's a famous seaside place called
    Blackpool,
    That's noted for fresh air and fun,
And Mr and Mrs Ramsbottom
    Went there with young Albert, their son.

A grand little lad was young Albert,
    All dressed in his best; quite a swell
With a stick with an 'orse's 'ead 'andle,
    The finest that Woolworth's could sell.

They didn't think much to the Ocean:
    The waves, they was fiddlin' and small,
There was no wrecks and nobody drownded,
    Fact, nothing to laugh at at all.

So, seeking for further amusement,
    They paid and went into the Zoo,
Where they'd Lions and Tigers and Camels,
    And old ale and sandwiches too.

There were one great big Lion called Wallace;
    His nose were all covered with scars
He lay in a somnolent posture,
    With the side of his face on the bars.

Now Albert had heard about Lions,
    How they was ferocious and wild
To see Wallace lying so peaceful,
    Well, it didn't seem right to the child.

So straightway the brave little feller,
    Not showing a morsel of fear,
Took his stick with its 'orse's 'ead 'andle
    And pushed it in Wallace's ear.

You could see that the Lion didn't like it,
    For giving a kind of a roll,
He pulled Albert inside the cage with 'im,
    And swallowed the little lad 'ole.

Then Pa, who had seen the occurrence,
    And didn't know what to do next,
Said 'Mother! Yon Lion's 'et Albert',
    And Mother said 'Well, I am vexed!'

Then Mr and Mrs Ramsbottom
    Quite rightly, when all's said and done,
Complained to the Animal Keeper,
    That the Lion had eaten their son.

The keeper was quite nice about it;
    He said 'What a nasty mishap.
Are you sure that it's your boy he's eaten?'
    Pa said 'Am I sure? There's his cap!'

The manager had to be sent for.
    He came and he said 'What's to do?'
Pa said 'Yon Lion's 'et Albert,
    And 'im in his Sunday clothes, too.'

Then Mother said, 'Right's right, young feller;
    I think it's a shame and a sin,
For a lion to go and eat Albert,
    And after we've paid to come in.'

The manager wanted no trouble,
    He took out his purse right away,
Saying 'How much to settle the matter?'
    And Pa said 'What do you usually pay?'

But Mother had turned a bit awkward
    When she thought where her Albert had gone.
She said 'No! someone's got to be summonsed'—
    So that was decided upon.

Then off they went to the P'lice Station,
    In front of the Magistrate chap;
They told 'im what happened to Albert,
    And proved it by showing his cap.

The Magistrate gave his opinion
    That no one was really to blame
And he said that he hoped the Ramsbottoms
    Would have further sons to their name.

At that Mother got proper blazing,
    'And thank you, sir, kindly,' said she.
'What waste all our lives raising children
    To feed ruddy Lions? Not me!'

Marriott Edgar

115

Activity 4

- Make your own dramatised reading of this poem with the voices of the Narrator, Mr and Mrs Ramsbottom, the Keeper and the Manager.

Unit 5

BALLADS

We came across ballads – stories in rhyme – in Part A. In this unit, we will look at ballads in more detail.

The ballad of *The Twa Corbies* tells of two carrion crows contemplating feeding off the body of a newly slain knight. Notice how all the images in the ballad are simple, direct, and imprint themselves on the mind's eye. The black crows, the white bones, the blue eyes and the golden hair are all very striking. It is a traditional Scottish ballad and is written in **dialect**.

The Twa Corbies*

*Two crows

As I was walking all alone,
I heard twa corbies making a moan:
The one unto the other say,
'Where shall we gang and dine today?'

'In behind yon auld fail* dyke   *turf
I wot there lies a new slain knight;
And nobody kens that he lies there,
But his hawk, his hound and his lady fair.

'His hound is to the hunting gane,
His hawk to fetch the wild fowl hame,
His lady's ta'en another mate,
So we may make our dinner sweet.

'Ye'll sit upon his white hause-bane*   *collar-bone
And I'll pike out his bonny blue een;
And with one lock of his golden hair
We'll theek* our nest when it grows bare.   *line

'Many a one for him makes moan,
But none shall ken where he is gone;
O'er his white bones when they are bare,
The wind shall blow for evermair.'

Anon

Activity 1

- Try reading the poem aloud. You could work in threes and have the voice of the narrator (at the beginning) and two crows. The first crow asks only 'Where shall we gang (go) and dine today?' but you could give the last two verses to the first crow instead of the second if you want to even up the reading. In some versions of the ballad, the lady remains faithful to her knight. What possible twist to the story does her taking 'another mate' suggest?

This next ballad is a conversation between a young man and the woman who is his dead lover who speaks to him from the grave. In some versions it is a young man who has been slain and his lover grieves for him.

The Unquiet Grave

'The wind doth blow today, my love,
 And a few small drops of rain;
I never had but one true-love,
 In a cold grave she was lain.

'I'll do as much for my true-love
 As any young man may;
I'll sit and mourn all at her grave
 For a twelvemonth and a day.'

The twelvemonth and a day being up,
 The dead began to speak:
'Oh who sits weeping on my grave,
 And will not let me sleep?'

''Tis I, my love, sits on your grave,
 And will not let you sleep;
For I crave one kiss of your clay-cold lips,
 And that is all I seek.'

'You crave one kiss of my clay-cold lips;
 But my breath smells earthy strong;
If you have one kiss of my clay-cold lips,
 Your time will not be long.

''Tis down in yonder garden green,
 Love, where we used to walk,
The finest flower that ere was seen
 Is withered to a stalk.

'The stalk is withered dry my love,
 So will our hearts decay;
So make yourself content, my love,
 Till God calls you away.'

Anon

Activity 2

- Read the poem *The Unquiet Grave.*

- What do you think is the message of the poem?

- In groups of three try to create your reading of the poem. You need voices for the young man, the narrator and the dead woman.

The Cherry-Tree Carol

Joseph was an old man,
    An old man was he
When he wedded Mary
    In the land of Galilee.

Joseph and Mary walking
    In the midst of a wood
Saw berries and cherries
    As red as the blood.

O then bespoke Mary,
    So meek and so mild,
'Pray get me one cherry,
    For I am with child.'

O then bespoke Joseph,
    So rude and unkind,
'Let him get thee a cherry
    That got thee with child.'

O then bespoke the babe
    Within his mother's womb,
'Bow down, thou tall cherry-tree,
    And give my mother some.'

Then bowed down the tall cherry-tree
    To his mother's right hand,
And she cried, 'See, Joseph,
    I have cherries at command!'

And Mary ate her cherry
    As red as the blood;
Then Mary went on
    With her heavy load.

Anon

Mother and Maiden

I sing of a maiden
    That is matchless.
King of all kings
    For her son she chose.

He came all so still
    Where his mother was,
As dew in April
    That falleth on the grass.

He came all so still
    To his mother's bower,
As dew in April
    That falleth on the flower.

He came all so still—
    There his mother lay,
As dew in April
    That falleth on the spray.

Mother and maiden
    Was never none but she;
Well may such a lady
    God's mother be.

Anon

The Demon Lover of the original story in the following poem was the ghost of a sailor to whom the woman in the poem had been betrothed. He drowned at sea and she married another man. After several years the ghost comes in human form to claim her as his wife. She is damned to hell for going to sea with him and the ship sinks.

This version suggests something altogether more demonic and theatrical from the husband having a cloven hoof to the magical ship with masts of gold and sails of taffeta.

The Demon Lover

'O where have you been, my long, long love,
    This long seven years and more?'
'O I'm come to seek my former vows
    Ye granted me before.'

'O hold your tongue of your former vows,
    For they will breed sad strife;
O hold your tongue of your former vows
    For I am become a wife.'

He turned him right and round about,
    And the tear blinded his ee:
'I would never hae trodden on Irish ground,
    If it had not been for thee.

'I might hae had a king's daughter,
    Far, far beyond the sea;
I might have had a king's daughter,
    Had it not been for love o' thee.'

'If ye might have had a king's daughter,
    Yeself ye had to blame;
Ye might have taken the king's daughter,
    For ye kend* that I was nane†.   *knew †none

'If I was to leave my husband dear,
    And my two babes also,
O what have you to take me to,
    If with you I should go?'

'I have seven ships upon the sea—
    And the eighth brought me to land—
With four-and-twenty bold mariners,
    And music on every hand.'

She has taken up her two little babes,
    Kissed them both cheek and chin:
'O fare ye well, my own two babes,
    For I'll never see you again.'

She set her foot upon the ship,
    No mariners could she behold;
But the sails were made of taffeta,
    And the masts of beaten gold.

She had not sailed a league, a league,
    A league but barely three,
When dismal grew his countenance,
    And drumlie* grew his ee†.   *gloomy, murky †eye

They had not sailed a league, a league,
    A league but barely three,
Until she espied his cloven foot,
    And she wept right bitterly.

'O hold your tongue of your weeping,' says he,
    'Of your weeping now let me be;
I will shew you how the lilies grow
    On the banks of Italy.'

'O what hills are yon, yon pleasant hills,
    That the sun shines sweetly on?'
'O yon are the hills of heaven,' he said,
    'Where you will never win.'

'O whaten* a mountain is yon,' she said,   *what sort of
    'All so dreary with frost and snow?'
'O yon is the mountain of hell,' he cried,
    'Where you and I will go.'

He struck the top-mast with his hand,
    The fore-mast with his knee,
And he broke that gallant ship in twain,
    And sank her in the sea.

Anon

Activity 3

- Prepare a reading of the poem. Three voices are needed – those of the young wife, the Demon Lover and the narrator.

In the next ballad a grisly nineteenth-century murder is re-told. Charlotte Dymond was a young Cornish girl who was allegedly murdered by her lover, Matthew, because he believed she loved someone else. Matthew was a cripple who could neither read nor write and there is some doubt as to whether or not he was actually guilty. Charles Causley uses the old ballad form when he re-tells her story.

The Ballad of Charlotte Dymond

It was a Sunday evening
And in the April rain
That Charlotte went from our house
And never came home again.

Her shawl of diamond redcloth
She wore a yellow gown,
She carried the green gauze handkerchief
She bought in Bodmin town.

About her throat her necklace
And in her purse her pay:
The four silver shillings
She had at Lady Day.

In her purse four shillings
And in her purse her pride.
As she walked out one evening
Her lover at her side.

Out beyond the marshes
Where the cattle stand,
With her crippled lover
Limping at her hand.

Charlotte walked with Matthew
Through the Sunday mist,
Never saw the razor
Waiting at his wrist.

Charlotte she was gentle
But they found her in the flood
Her Sunday beads among the reeds
Beaming with her blood.

Matthew, where is Charlotte,
And wherefore has she flown?
For you walked out together
And now are come alone.

Why do you not answer,
Stand silent as a tree,
Your Sunday worsted stockings
All muddied to the knee?

Why do you mend your breast-pleat
With a rusty needle's thread
And fall with fears and silent tears
Upon your single bed?

Why do you sit so sadly
Your face the colour of clay
And with a green gauze handkerchief
Wipe the sour sweat away?

Has she gone to Blisland
To seek an easier place?
And is that why your eye won't dry
And blinds your bleaching face?

'Take me home!' cried Charlotte,
'I lie here in the pit!
A red rock rests upon my breasts
And my naked neck is split!'

Her skin was soft as sable
Her eyes were wide as day,
Her hair was blacker than the bog
That licked her life away.

Her cheeks were made of honey,
Her throat was made of flame
Where all around the razor
Had written its red name.

As Matthew turned at Plymouth
About the tilting Hoe,
The cold and cunning Constable
Up to him did go.

'I've come to take you, Matthew,
Unto the Magistrate's door.
Come quiet now, you pretty poor boy,
And you must know what for.'

'She is as pure,' cried Matthew,
'As is the early dew,
Her only stain it is the pain
That round her neck I drew!

'She is as guiltless as the day
She sprang forth from her mother.
The only sin upon her skin
Is that she loved another.'

They took him off to Bodmin,
They pulled the prison bell,
They sent him smartly up to heaven
And dropped him down to Hell.

All through the granite kingdom
And on its travelling airs
Ask which of these two lovers
The most deserves your prayers.

And your steel heart search, Stranger
That you may pause and pray
For lovers who come not to bed
Upon their wedding day.

But lie upon the moorland
Where stands the sacred snow
Above the breathing river,
And the salt sea-winds go.

Charles Causley

Activity 4

- Read the poem through once and then, in groups, divide up the poem and produce your own reading of it with different voices taking different parts.

- You can find a great deal of background information about the murder of Charlotte Dymond on a number of websites. Reading the poem and the background information, you will realise that Charlotte's story is sadly similar to so many stories that appear in newspapers every week.

- With this in mind, you might tackle writing your own ballad. Take an appropriate story from a newspaper and try to tell it simply in verses of four lines each. Aim to make the last words of the second and fourth lines rhyme in each verse if you can.

Robert Burns' poem *John Barleycorn* is not about a man at all but about the stages in growing and harvesting barley and the processes by which it is made into other products, such as beer, bread and, perhaps most significantly, whisky.

John Barleycorn

There were three kings into the east,
   Three kings both great and high;
And they hae sworn a solemn oath
   John Barleycorn should die.

They took a plough and plough'd him down,
   Put clods upon his head;
And they hae sworn a solemn oath
   John Barleycorn was dead.

But the cheerful Spring came kindly on,
   And show'rs began to fall;
John Barleycorn got up again,
   And sore surpris'd them all.

The sultry suns of Summer came,
   And he grew thick and strong;
His head weel arm'd wi' pointed spears,
   That no one should him wrong.

The sober Autumn enter'd mild,
   When he grew wan and pale;
His bending joints and drooping head
   Show'd he began to fail.

His colour sicken'd more and more,
   He faded into age;
And then his enemies began
   To show their deadly rage.

They've ta'en a weapon, long and sharp,
    And cut him by the knee;
Then tied him fast upon a cart,
    Like a rogue for forgerie.

They laid him down upon his back,
    And cudgell'd him full sore;
They hung him up before the storm,
    And turn'd him o'er and o'er.

They filléd up a darksome pit
    With water to the brim;
They heavéd in John Barleycorn,
    There let him sink or swim.

They laid him out upon the floor,
    To work him further woe;
And still, as signs of life appear'd,
    They toss'd him to and fro.

They wasted o'er a scorching flame
    The marrow of his bones;
But a miller us'd him worst of all—
    He crush'd him 'tween two stones.

And they hae ta'en his very heart's blood,
    And drank it round and round;
And still the more and more they drank,
    Their joy did more abound.

John Barleycorn was a hero bold,
    Of noble enterprise;
For if you do but taste his blood,
    'Twill make your courage rise.

'Twill make a man forget his woe;
    'Twill heighten all his joy;
'Twill make the widow's heart to sing,
    Tho' the tear were in her eye.

Then let us toast John Barleycorn,
    Each man a glass in hand;
And may his great posterity
    Ne'er fail in old Scotland.

Robert Burns

Activity 5

- John Barleycorn is a **personification** of barley.
  - What do the opening lines make you think of?
  - Are there any other ideas in the poem that might suggest something similar?
  - What stages can you identify in John Barleycorn's life and death?
- Prepare a reading of the poem using several voices one for each verse, or splitting it into sections. Try to suit the way you read to the ideas in each verse, e.g. positive and strong in spring and summer, increasingly sickly and weak in autumn, cruel for the pains he endures and triumphant at the end.

Unit 6
CREATURES

The character and behaviour of animals are favourite subjects for poets. Poems have been written about every imaginable creature and in many different ways.

William Blake's *The Tyger* is probably one of the best-known poems in the English language. He wrote the poem and drew the picture that accompanies it. The poem consists of a series of questions, which, in a way, are all the same question.

The Tyger

Tyger Tyger, burning bright,
In the forests of the night;
What immortal hand or eye,
Could frame thy fearful symmetry?

In what distant deeps or skies,
Burnt the fire of thine eyes?
On what wings dare he aspire?
What the hand dare seize the fire?

And what shoulder, & what art,
Could twist the sinews of thy heart?
And when thy heart began to beat,
What dread hand? & what dread feet?

What the hammer? what the chain,
In what furnace was thy brain?
What the anvil? what dread grasp,
Dare its deadly terrors clasp?

When the stars threw down their spears,
And watered heaven with their tears:
Did he smile his work to see?
Did he who made the Lamb make thee?

Tyger! Tyger! burning bright,
In the forests of the night:
What immortal hand or eye,
Dare frame thy fearful symmetry?

William Blake

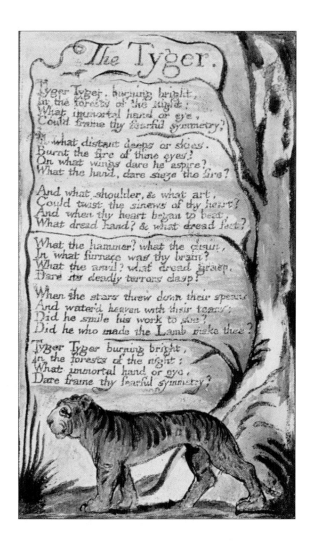

Activity 1

- Read the poem.
- In pairs, decide what each of the questions in the poem is asking.
- What is the biggest question of all?

To a Mouse

On Turning her up in her Nest with the Plough

Wee, sleekit*, cow'rin, tim'rous beastie,	*sleek and dainty
O what a panic's in thy breastie!	
Thou need na start awa sae hasty,	
Wi' bickering brattle*!	*with a panicked scurry/scamper
I wad be laith* to rin an' chase thee,	*loath, unwilling
Wi' murd'ring pattle*!	*a small spade used to clean a plough

I'm truly sorry man's dominion
Has broken nature's social union
An' justifies that ill opinion
Which makes thee startle
At me, thy poor, earth-born companion,
An' fellow-mortal!

I doubt na, whiles*, but thou may thieve;	*sometimes
What then? poor beastie, thou maun* live!	*must
A daimen-icker in a thrave*	*an occasional ear of corn in 24 sheaves
'S a sma' request:	
I'll get a blessin wi' the lave*,	*remainder
An' never miss't!	

Thy wee-bit housie, too, in ruin!	
Its silly wa's the win's are strewin!	
An' naething, now, to big* a new ane,	*build
O' foggage* green!	*moss
An' bleak December's winds ensuin,	
Baith* snell† an' keen!	*both †biting

126

Thou saw the fields laid bare an' waste
An' weary Winter comin fast,
An' cozie here, beneath the blast,
Thou thought to dwell,
Till, crash! the cruel coulter* past   *sharp cutting blade of a plough
Out thro' thy cell.

That wee-bit heap o' leaves an' stibble*   *stubble/bits of straw
Has cost thee mony* a weary nibble!   *many
Now thou's turn'd out, for a' thy trouble,
But house or hald*,   *without a home
To thole* the winter's sleety dribble,   *endure
An' cranreuch* cauld†!   *hoar-frost †cold

But Mousie, thou art no thylane*   *you are not alone
In proving foresight may be vain:
The best laid schemes o' Mice an' Men,
Gang aft a-gley*,   *often go wrong
An' lea'e us nought but grief an' pain,
For promis'd joy!

Still, thou art blest, compar'd wi' me!
The present only toucheth thee:
But oh! I backward cast my e'e*,   *eye
On prospects drear!
An' forward, tho' I canna see,
I guess an' fear!

Robert Burns

Activity 2

- Hear the poem read aloud.
- In pairs or small groups try to give a clear account of the story that Burns tells.
- What is his conclusion in the last verse?
- What impression do you have of the poet from this poem?

In the next poem, the poet tells of two people stopping high in a snowy mountain pasture when they see a little Morgan colt. Morgans are a famously tough, friendly breed of horse but this one is still very young and fearful of the snow.

The Runaway

Once when the snow of the year was beginning to fall,
We stopped by a mountain pasture to say, 'Whose colt?'
A little Morgan had one forefoot on the wall,
The other curled at his breast. He dipped his head
And snorted at us. And then he had to bolt.
We heard the miniature thunder where he fled,
And saw him, or thought we saw him, dim and grey,
Like a shadow against the curtain of falling flakes.
'I think the little fellow's afraid of the snow.
He isn't winter-broken. It isn't play
With the little fellow at all. He's running away.
I doubt if even his mother could tell him, "Sakes,
It's only weather." He'd think she didn't know!
Where is his mother? He can't be out alone.'
And now he comes again with clatter of stone,
And mounts the wall again with whited eyes
And all his tail that isn't hair up straight.
He shudders his coat as if to throw off flies.
'Whoever it is that leaves him out so late,
When other creatures have gone to stall and bin,
Ought to be told to come and take him in.'

Robert Frost

Activity 3

- Read the poem and hear the conversation about the colt.
- What tells the poet that the colt isn't used to snow and is frightened?
- What does he feel its owners should do?
- What does this suggest to you about the poet?
- Imagine you happened upon the same scene as the poet. Describe in detail, as though in a diary entry, exactly what you saw.

First Sight

Lambs that learn to walk in snow
When their bleating clouds the air
Meet a vast unwelcome, know
Nothing but a sunless glare.
Newly stumbling to and fro
All they find, outside the fold,
Is a wretched width of cold.

As they wait beside the ewe,
Her fleeces wetly caked, there lies
Hidden round them, waiting too,
Earth's immeasurable surprise.
They could not grasp it if they knew,
What so soon will wake and grow
Utterly unlike the snow.

Philip Larkin

Warning to a Worm

An alimentary tract
    undressed in flesh and bone
    should not be out alone;
that's elementary fact.

Go home, small hoover-pipe:
    go home, elastic hose
    that lacks a leg, that grows
and then contracts its shape.

Segmented, tapered tube:
    twin-ended tentacle:
    go home, small article
of food, before birds grab

and eat you. Hurry. Rush.
Beware the savage Thrush.

Anna Adams

129

Activity 4

- Read the two poems.
- What is the 'immeasurable surprise' that awaits the new-born lambs in the last three lines of Larkin's poem?
- In *Warning to a Worm*, there are several comparisons. Which ones appeal to you most and why?
- Both poems are variations on a familiar form. To discover which one, on clean copies of the poems mark the rhyme schemes at the end of each line using different letters. Then, mark the stress pattern with a / to indicate the regular beat of the lines.

Activity 5

- The 8 lines of this two-verse poem are printed in random order. Without looking at a correct version, can you put them in the correct order? Cover up the correct version below before you start work!

The Eagle

Round the hill-side,
Scanning the ground to kill.
He looks as though from his own wings
He hangs between his wings outspread
And bends a narrow golden head,
Level and still
He hung down crucified.
Yet as he sails and smoothly swings

Andrew Young

- When you have unscrambled the poem, in pairs discuss:
  - What picture do you get of the eagle in flight?
  - What is the contrast in the last lines of each verse?

The actual poem is shown below.

The Eagle

He hangs between his wings outspread
    Level and still
And bends a narrow golden head,
    Scanning the ground to kill.

Yet as he sails and smoothly swings
    Round the hill-side,
He looks as though from his own wings
    He hung down crucified.

Andrew Young

Richard Kell's poem *Pigeons* is full of details about how town pigeons move, what they look like and the sounds they make. Throughout the poem he is comparing the pigeons to other things – they strut 'like fat gentlemen', their heads are 'like tiny hammers' tapping 'imaginary nails'. These comparisons help us see the picture of the pigeons more clearly in our mind's eye.

Pigeons

They paddle with staccato feet
In powder-pools of sunlight,
Small blue busybodies
Strutting like fat gentlemen
With hands clasped
Under their swallowtail coats;
And, as they stump about,
Their heads like tiny hammers
Tap at imaginary nails
In non-existent walls.
Elusive ghosts of sunshine
Slither down the green gloss
Of their necks an instant, and are gone.

Summer hangs drugged from sky to earth
In limpid fathoms of silence:
Only warm dark dimples of sound
Slide like slow bubbles
From the contented throats.

Raise a casual hand–
With one quick gust
They fountain into air.

Richard Kell

Activity 6

- Read the poem.

- Now choose a creature – something you can imagine clearly. It may be a pet cat or dog, a budgie or a goldfish, a gerbil or a hamster. Or it may be something you might see in the wild – a hawk hovering and swooping after prey, a pike darting after smaller fish, a crab on the seashore. Concentrate on its movement – what words best describe it? What is it *like*? Concentrate on its appearance – what words best describe it? What is it *like*? Concentrate on any sound it may make – what words best describe it? What is it *like*?

- Write down your ideas. Look back at what you have written. Try to shape your ideas into a poem that describes what you see and feel.

Talking Turkeys!!

Be nice to yu turkeys dis christmas
Cos turkeys jus wanna hav fun
Turkeys are cool, turkeys are wicked
An every turkey has a Mum.
Be nice to yu turkeys dis christmas,
Don't eat it, keep it alive,
It could be yu mate an not on yu plate
Say, Yo! Turkey I'm on your side.

I got lots of friends who are turkeys
An all of dem fear christmas time,
Dey say 'Benj man, eh, I wanna enjoy it,
But dose humans destroyed it
An humans are out of dere mind,
Yeah, I got lots of friends who are turkeys
Dey all hav a right to a life,
Not to be caged up an genetically made up
By any farmer an his wife.

Turkeys jus wanna play reggae
Turkeys jus wanna hip-hop
Have you ever seen a nice young turkey
    saying,
'I cannot wait for de chop'?
Turkeys like getting presents, dey wanna
    watch christmas TV,
Turkeys hav brains an turkeys feel pain
In many ways like yu an me.

I once knew a turkey His name was Turkey
He said 'Benji explain to me please,
Who put de turkey in christmas
An what happens to christmas trees?'
I said, 'I am not too sure Turkey
But it's nothing to do wid Christ Mass
Humans get greedy and waste more dan
    need be
An business men mek loadsa cash.'

So, be nice to yu turkey dis christmas
Invite dem indoors fe sum greens
Let dem eat cake an let dem partake
In a plate of organic grown beans,
Be nice to yu turkey dis christmas
An spare dem de cut of de knife,
Join Turkeys United an dey'll be delighted
An yu will mek new friends 'FOR LIFE'.

Benjamin Zephaniah

Activity 7

- As a group, read the poem together.
- Ask yourself what the poem is about. Has the poet got a point?

Woodpecker

Woodpecker is rubber-necked
    But has a nose of steel.
He bangs his head against the wall
    And cannot even feel.

When Woodpecker's jack-hammer head
    Starts up its dreadful din
Knocking the dead bough double dead
    How do his eyes stay in?

Pity the poor dead oak that cries
    In terrors and in pains.
But pity more Woodpecker's eyes
    And bouncing rubber brains.

Ted Hughes

Activity 8

Ted Hughes' *Woodpecker* has a quite different sound and movement from John Agard's on page **28**. Hear this poem read aloud and listen for the rhythm.

- What gives the verses their jaunty repeated rhythm? You may find it helps to count the syllables in each line and to tap out the rhythm with a finger as you say it.

- Can you see a pattern?

Cat

cold white cat
waiting
in the lamplight
floodlit
in the dark night
always watching
always waiting
green-eyed and strange
for my return.
the distance
between us
is infinite
you content
in the immediacy
of the cold night
me seeking security
behind a darkened door.
you never purr
or move towards me
to rub against my ankles
but watch and wait
whilst I hurry down the street
fumble for my key
and enter the house.
I shut you out
but you're always there
each morning
each evening
the consciousness
within
my sleep.

Sue Kelly

Ode On the Death of A Favourite Cat Drowned in a Tub of Gold Fishes

'Twas on a lofty vase's side,
Where China's gayest art had dyed
The azure* flowers that blow;   *blue
Demurest of the tabby kind,
The pensive Selima reclin'd,
Gaz'd on the lake below.

Her conscious tail her joy declared;
The fair round face, the snowy beard,
The velvet of her paws,
Her coat, that with the tortoise vies,
Her ears of jet, and emerald eyes,
She saw: and purred applause.

Still had she gazed; but 'midst the tide
Two angel forms were seen to glide,
The Genii* of the stream;   *spirits
Their scaly armour's Tyrian* hue,   *purple
Thro' richest purple, to the view,
Betray'd a golden gleam.

The hapless Nymph with wonder saw:
A whisker first, and then a claw,
With many an ardent wish,
She stretched, in vain, to reach the prize.
What female heart can gold despise?
What cat's averse to fish?

Presumptuous maid! with looks intent
Again she stretched, again she bent,
Nor knew the gulf between;
(Malignant Fate sat by, and smiled.)
The slippery verge her feet beguiled;
She tumbled headlong in.

Eight times emerging from the flood,
She mew'd to every watery God,
Some speedy aid to send.
No Dolphin came, no Nereid* stirred; *sea nymph
Nor cruel Tom, nor Susan heard.
A favourite has no friend.

134

From hence, ye beauties, undeceived,
Know, one false step is ne'er retrieved,
And be with caution bold.
Not all that tempts your wandering eyes
And heedless hearts, is lawful prize,
Nor all, that glisters, gold.

Thomas Gray

Activity 9

Gray's poem records an actual event when the cat belonging to his friend Horace Walpole, was sadly drowned in a vase.

- Read the poem.

- In the first three verses, what strikes you about the language used?

- What change appears to be coming over the cat in verses 4 and 5?

- What is the moral of the poem? Is it to do with cats?

The Kitten and Falling Leaves

See the kitten on the wall
Sporting with the leaves that fall,
Withered leaves – one – two – and three –
From the lofty elder tree!

– But the kitten, how she starts,
Crouches, stretches, paws, and darts!
First at one, and then its fellow
Just as light and just as yellow;
There are many now – now one –
Now they stop and there are none.

What intenseness of desire
In her upward eye of fire!
With a tiger-leap half way
Now she meets the coming prey,
Let it go as fast, and then
Has it in her power again:
Now she works with three or four,
Like an Indian conjurer,
Quick as he in feats of art,
Far beyond the joy of heart...

William Wordsworth

Hatching

His night has come to an end and now he
       must break
The little sky which shielded him. He taps
Once and nothing happens. He tries again
And makes a mark like lightning. He must
       thunder,
Storm and shake and break a universe
Too small and safe. His daring beak does this.

And now he is out in a world of smells and
       spaces.
He shivers. Any air is wind to him.
He huddles under wings but does not know
He is already shaping feathers for
A lunge into the sky. His solo flight
Will bring the sun upon his back. He'll bear
       it,
Carry it, learn the real winds, by instinct
Return for food and, larger than his mother,
Avid for air, harry her with his hunger.

Elizabeth Jennings

The Spider Holds a Silver Ball

The Spider holds a Silver Ball
In unperceived Hands –
And dancing softly to Himself
His Yarn of Pearl – unwinds –

He plies from Nought to Nought –
In unsubstantial trade –
Supplants our Tapestries with His –
In half the period –

An Hour to rear supreme
His Continents of Light –
Then dangle from the Housewife's Broom –
His Boundaries – forgot –

Emily Dickinson

Death of a Naturalist

All year the flax-dam festered in the heart
Of the townland; green and heavy headed
Flax had rotted there, weighted down by huge sods.
Daily it sweltered in the punishing sun.
Bubbles gargled delicately, bluebottles
Wove a strong gauze of sound around the smell.
There were dragon-flies, spotted butterflies,
But best of all was the warm thick slobber
Of frogspawn that grew like clotted water
In the shade of the banks. Here, every spring
I would fill jampotfuls of the jellied
Specks to range on window-sills at home,
On shelves at school, and wait and watch until
The fattening dots burst into nimble-
Swimming tadpoles. Miss Walls would tell us how
The daddy frog was called a bullfrog
And how he croaked and how the mammy frog
Laid hundreds of little eggs and this was
Frogspawn. You could tell the weather by frogs too
For they were yellow in the sun and brown
In rain.

   Then one hot day when fields were rank
With cowdung in the grass the angry frogs
Invaded the flax-dam; I ducked through hedges
To a coarse croaking that I had not heard
Before. The air was thick with a bass chorus.
Right down the dam gross-bellied frogs were cocked
On sods; their loose necks pulsed like sails. Some hopped:
The slap and plop were obscene threats. Some sat
Poised like mud grenades, their blunt heads farting.
I sickened, turned, and ran. The great slime kings
Were gathered there for vengeance and I knew
That if I dipped my hand the spawn would clutch it.

Seamus Heaney

Unit 7

SCHOOL

Miroslav Holub's poem *A Boy's Head* imagines some of the very strange and varied things that might take up space in a young boy's mind.

A Boy's Head

In it there is a space-ship
and a project
for doing away with piano lessons.

And there is
Noah's ark,
which shall be first.

And there is
an entirely new bird,
an entirely new hare,
an entirely new bumble-bee.

There is a river
that flows upwards.

There is a multiplication table.

There is anti-matter.

And it just cannot be trimmed.

I believe
that only what cannot be trimmed
is a head.
There is much promise
in the circumstance
that so many people have heads.

Miroslav Holub

(trans. I. Milner and G. Theiner)

Activity 1

- Read the poem.
- Do you think the poet is right or would you suggest other items and ideas are more likely to occupy his mind?
- Would the things that occupy a girl's mind be the same?
- What does he suggest in the last two sentences of the poem?
- *Either* make a list of the nine or ten things you think might be in a boy's head and write your own version of the poem,
- *Or* list items that might occupy a girl's mind and write your own poem as a sequel entitled *A Girl's Head*.

Term Begins Again
(Ostrich Blues)

I find myself
in bed again
with the sheets up over
my head again

papers collect
on my desk again
reports and memos and lists again

there are the
timetables in black ink
again

the silhouetted heads
in rows against the light
again

the lists again
of books I haven't read
again

nightmares again
of assignations missed
again

of students riding off
on bicycles playing bass guitars
again

and I oversleep

again
and again

I find myself
in bed
again

with the sheets up over
my head

again

Stef Pixner

Activity 2

The poem captures the feelings of a teacher who is as unwilling to go to school at the beginning of a new term, as are some of her students.

- Read the poem.

- Why does she call it a 'blues'?

- Why *Ostrich* blues?

- What is the most frequently used word in the poem? What is the effect of the repetition?

- Are this teacher's feelings at the beginning of term anything like yours?

- Choose something similar that you dread. It might be the beginning of term, but it might be Monday mornings (or any particular dreaded day), or it might be a particular lesson, and write your own Blues.

Tich Miller

Tich Miller wore glasses
with elastoplast-pink frames
and had one foot three sizes larger than
      the other.

When they picked the teams for outdoor
      games
she and I were always the last two
left standing by the wire-mesh fence.

We avoided one another's eyes,
stooping, perhaps, to re-tie a shoelace,
or affecting interest in the flight

of some fortunate bird, and pretended
not to hear the urgent conference:
'Have Tubby!' 'No, no, have Tich!'

Usually they chose me, the lesser dud,
and she lolloped, unselected,
to the back of the othe team.

At eleven we went off to different schools.
In time I learned to get my own back,
sneering at hockey-players who couldn't
      spell.

Tich died when she was twelve.

Wendy Cope

Exercise Book

Two and two four
four and four eight
eight and eight sixteen...
Once again! says the master
Two and two four
four and four eight
eight and eight sixteen.
But look! the lyre bird
high on the wing
the child sees it
the child hears it
the child calls it
Save me
play with me
bird!
So the bird alights
and plays with the child
Two and two four...
Once again! says the master
and the child plays
and the bird plays too...
Four and four eight
eight and eight sixteen
and twice sixteen makes what?
Twice sixteen makes nothing
least of all thirty-two
anyhow
and off they go

For the child has hidden
The bird in his desk
and all the children
hear its song
and all the children
hear the music
and eight and eight in their turn
off they go
and four and four and two and two
in their turn fade away
and one and one make neither one nor two

but one by one off they go.
And the lyre-bird sings
and the child sings
and the master shouts
When you've quite finished playing the fool!
But all the children
Are listening to the music
And the walls of the classroom
quietly crumble.
The window panes turn
once more to sand
the ink is sea
the desk is trees
the chalk is cliffs
and the quill pen
a bird again.

Paul Dehn

Activity 3

- Read the poem *Exercise Book* and decide what you think the poem is about.

- Prepare a group reading of the poem. Decide which lines should be chanted together as a group and which ones need an individual voice.

In her poem *In Mrs Tilscher's Class*, Carol Ann Duffy remembers fragments of her primary schooldays in the 1960s. Although the day-to-day details of classrooms have changed since then, maybe the feelings of some year 6 girls at the end of primary school are not so very different now.

In Mrs Tilscher's Class

You could travel up the Blue Nile
with your finger, tracing the route
while Mrs Tilscher chanted the scenery.
Tana. Ethiopia. Khartoum. Aswân.
That for an hour, then a skittle of milk
and the chalky Pyramids rubbed into dust.
A window opened with a long pole.
The laugh of a bell swung by a running child.

This was better than home. Enthralling books.
The classroom glowed like a sweet shop.
Sugar paper. Coloured shapes. Brady and Hindley
faded, like the faint, uneasy smudge of a mistake.
Mrs Tilscher loved you. Some mornings, you found
she'd left a good gold star by your name.
The scent of a pencil slowly, carefully, shaved.
A xylophone's nonsense heard from another form.

Over the Easter term, the inky tadpoles changed
from commas into exclamation marks. Three frogs
hopped in the playground, freed by a dunce,
followed by a line of kids, jumping and croaking
away from the lunch queue. A rough boy
told you how you were born. You kicked him, but stared
at your parents, appalled, when you got back home.

That feverish July, the air tasted of electricity.
A tangible alarm made you always untidy, hot,
fractious under the heavy, sexy sky. You asked her
how you were born and Mrs Tilscher smiled,
then turned away. Reports were handed out.
You ran through the gates, impatient to be grown,
as the sky split open into a thunderstorm.

Carol Ann Duffy

Activity 4

- Share some of your most vivid memories of being at primary school.

- Hear the poem read aloud. Concentrate on the words and the pictures they conjure up in your mind.

  - In the first verse, what is Mrs Tilscher doing?

  - What do you think 'a skittle of milk' might be? Why is this a good description?

  - What kind of Pyramids were they and what happened to them after break?

  - How would you describe the atmosphere of this primary classroom? How did the writer feel about being in Mrs Tilscher's class?

  - Who were 'Brady and Hindley' and why, in this world, do they seem 'a mistake'?

  - Reading the last two verses together, what seems to be the main thing on the girl's mind? What prompts this?

Roger McGough's poem, *The Railings*, is about his own experience as a teenager at St Mary's College, a catholic grammar school in Liverpool.

The Railings

You came to watch me playing cricket once.
Quite a few of the fathers did.
At ease, outside the pavilion
they would while away a Saturday afternoon.
Joke with the masters, urge on
their flannelled offspring. But not you.

Fielding deep near the boundary
I saw you through the railings.
You were embarrassed when I waved
and moved out of sight down the road.
When it was my turn to bowl though
I knew you'd still be watching.

Third ball, a wicket, and three more followed.
When we came in at the end of the innings
the other dads applauded and joined us for tea.
Of course, you had gone by then. Later,
you said you'd found yourself there by accident.
Just passing. Spotted me through the railings.

* * *

Speech-days . Prize givings . School-plays
The Twentyfirst . The Wedding . The Christening
You would find yourself there by accident.
Just passing. Spotted me through the railings.

Roger McGough

Activity 5

- Read the poem.

- Roger McGough's father was a Liverpool docker who left school at 14. Why do you think he didn't like to be noticed when he watched his son?

- So, why *did* he watch him then? What do you think his feelings might have been?

- There were real railings round the cricket ground but not at the other important events in the poet's life – speech-days, prize-givings, school-plays, the twenty-first birthday, the wedding, the christening. What sort of railings were these?

In her poem, *Timetable*, Kate Clanchy gives us a memory of her schooldays a generation ago.

Timetable

We all remember school, of course:
the lino warming, shoe bag smell, expanse
of polished floor. It's where we learned
to wait: hot cheeked in class, dreaming,
bored, for cheesy milk, for noisy now.
We learned to count, to rule off days,
and pattern time in coloured squares:
purple English, dark green Maths.

We hear the bells, sometimes,
for years, the squeal and crack
of chalk on black. We walk, don't run,
in awkward pairs, hoping for the open door,
a foreign teacher, fire drill. And love
is long aertex summers, tennis sweat,
and somewhere, someone singing flat.
The art room, empty, full of light.

Kate Clanchy

Activity 6

- Talk about the poem and then try to answer these questions:
    - 'It's where we learned to wait,' she says of school. What were they waiting for?
    - Do you see a connection between this idea and one in Carol Ann Duffy's poem?

Simon Armitage's poem *Learning by Rote* (which means 'learning in a mechanical manner without understanding') is printed almost entirely with the letters reversed as in a mirror.

Learning by Rote

Dear Sir, in class I was the backwards boy
who wrote cack-handedly. You made me sign
my name – but in reverse – ten thousand times.
Because the punishment must fit the crime.

Simon Armitage, Simon Armitage
at break time, after school, four thousand, five,
Simon Armitage, Simon Armitage
eight thousand, nine, until my father's note:

Enough's enough. Now leave the boy alone.

Forgotten. Buried in the past. Except
this loose-leaf jotter came to light today,
crammed with some Latin-looking motto, page
on page on page on page, the words

Simon Armitage, Simon Armitage

and then the sudden, childish urge to wave
this wad of mirror-writing in your face.
And then again, and then again, and then
again, again, again, again.

Simon Armitage

Activity 7

- Try to decipher the poem then hear it read aloud.
- Discuss:
  - Who is the 'Dear Sir' in the first line?
  - What do the phrases 'the backwards boy' and 'cack-handedly' tell you about the schoolboy Simon? Does it help explain why he prints the poem as he does?
  - How and why was he punished?
  - Who caused the punishment to end?
  - Why does the adult Simon have the urge to wave the mass of mirror writing that he has come across from his schooldays right in the face of 'Dear Sir' again and again...?

Activity 6

- Write down, for about five minutes, some of the memories and impressions you have from your own junior schooldays. You could concentrate *either* on your primary school *or* the first days at secondary school. What sounds, images, smells do you remember? What voices? What games? What lessons? What was positive and what was not?

- From your jumble of ideas and impressions see if you can begin to shape your poem about life as you recall it in, for example, Mrs X's class. Remember to concentrate on tiny details as well as on big things. Tiny details –'The scent of a pencil carefully shaved/ A xylophone's nonsense heard from another form' – are the sort of things that make us stop and say 'That's right: I remember that...'

Unit 8

ME

Going Through the Old Photos

Me, my dad
and my brother
we were looking through the old photos.
Pictures of my dad with a broken leg
and my mum with big flappy shorts on
and me on a tricycle
when we got to one of my mum
with a baby on her knee,
and I go,
'Is that me or Brian?'
And my dad says,
'Let's have a look.
It isn't you or Brian,' he says.
'It's Alan.
He died.
He would have been
two years younger than Brian
and two years older than you.
He was a lovely baby.'

'How did he die?'
'Whooping cough.
I was away at the time.
He coughed himself to death in Connie's
    arms.
The terrible thing is,
it wouldn't happen today,
but it was during the war, you see,
and they didn't have the medicines.
That must be the only photo
of him we've got.'

Me and Brian
looked at the photo.
We couldn't say anything.
It was the first time we had ever heard about
    Alan.
For a moment I felt ashamed
like as if I had done something wrong.

I looked at the baby trying to work out
who he looked like.
I wanted to know what another brother
would have been like.
No way of saying.
And Mum looked so happy.
Of course she didn't know
when they took the photo
that he would die, did she?

Funny thing is,
though my father mentioned it every now
    and then
over the years,
Mum—never.
And he never said anything in front of her
about it
and we never let on that we knew.
What I've never figured out
was whether
her silence was because
she was more upset about it
than my dad—
or less.

Michael Rosen

148

Activity 1

- Trace the changing feelings that the poem records as the story of Alan's brief life is told.
  - What are the two boys' feelings at the end of section 1?
  - What are the father's feelings at the end of section 2?
  - What are the boys' feelings at lines 5 and 6 in section 3?
  - In the last section, how do different members of the family react to the knowledge of the baby's death and why?
- Find one or more of your family photographs, probably with happier associations than Michael Rosen's, and write your own poem about the memories and feelings you are reminded of.
- Scan your photographs and create your own photograph/poem combination.

Not Yet My Mother

Yesterday I found a photo
of you at seventeen,
holding a horse and smiling,
not yet my mother.

The tight riding hat hid your hair,
and your legs were still the long shins of a
    boy's.
You held the horse by the halter,
your hand a fist under its huge jaw.

The blown trees were still in the background
and the sky was grained by the old film stock,
but what caught me was your face,
which was mine.

And I thought, just for a second, that you
    were me.
But then I saw the woman's jacket,
nipped at the waist, the ballooned jodhpurs,
and of course, the date scratched in the
    corner.

All of which told me again,
that this was you at seventeen, holding a
    horse
and smiling, not yet my mother,
although I was clearly already your child.

Owen Sheers

Activity 2

The poem, *Not Yet My Mother*, is about looking at an old photograph, just like the one previously. The poet finds a picture of the girl who was later to become his mother. She was seventeen when the picture was taken.

- What surprises him most about the photograph?
- What do you think the poet means by the last two lines of his poem?

Childhood

I used to think that grown-up people chose
To have stiff backs and wrinkles round their nose,
And veins like small fat snakes on either hand,
On purpose to be grand.
Till through the banisters I watched one day
My great-aunt Etty's friend who was going away,
And how her onyx beads had come unstrung.
I saw her grope to find them as they rolled;
And then I knew that she was helplessly old,
As I was helplessly young.

Frances Cornford

Old People

Why are people impatient when they are old?
Is it because they are tired of trying to make
Fast things move slowly?
I have seen their eyes flinch as they watch lorries
Lurching and hurrying past.
I have also seen them twitch and move away
When a grandbaby cries.
They can go to the cinema cheaply,
They can do what they like all day.
Yet they shrink and shiver, looking like old, used dolls.
I do not think that I should like to be old.

Elizabeth Jennings

Warning

When I am an old woman I shall wear purple
With a red hat that doesn't go and doesn't suit me.
And I shall spend my pension on brandy and summer gloves
And satin sandals and say we've no money for butter.
I shall sit down on the pavement when I'm tired
And gobble up samples in shops and press alarm bells
And run my stick along the public railings
And make up for the sobriety of my youth.
I shall go out in my slippers in the rain
And pick flowers in other people's gardens
And learn to spit.

You can wear terrible shirts and grow more fat
And eat three pounds of sausages at a go
Or only eat bread and pickle for a week
And hoard pens and pencils and beermats and things in boxes.

But now we must have clothes that keep us dry
And pay our rent and not swear in the street
And set a good example for the children.
We must have friends to dinner and read the papers.

But maybe I ought to practise a little now?
So people who know me are not too shocked and surprised
When suddenly I am old and start to wear purple.

Jenny Joseph

Activity 3

Frances Cornford's poem *Childhood* and Elizabeth Jenning's poem *Old People* both suggest old age may be a sad time. Jenny Joseph's poem *Warning* suggests something quite different.

- How do you see old age? A terrible burden? Something that can be enjoyed?

- Write down the first ideas that come to mind when you finish the sentence 'Being old is...' and see if you can shape a poem of your own from your ideas.

Life Doesn't Frighten Me

Shadows on the wall
Noises down the hall
Life doesn't frighten me at all
Bad dogs barking loud
Big ghosts in a cloud
Life doesn't frighten me at all.

Mean old Mother Goose
Lions on the loose
They don't frighten me at all
Dragons breathing flame
On my counterpane
That doesn't frighten me at all.

I go boo
Make them shoo
I make fun
Way them run
I won't cry
So they fly
I just smile
They go wild
Life doesn't frighten me at all.

Tough guys in a fight
All alone at night
Life doesn't frighten me at all.
Panthers in the park
Strangers in the dark
No, they don't frighten me at all.

That new classroom where
Boys all pull my hair
(Kissy little girls
With their hair in curls)
They don't frighten me at all.

Don't show me frogs and snakes
And listen for my scream,
If I'm afraid at all
It's only in my dreams.

I've got a magic charm
That I keep up my sleeve,
I can walk the ocean floor
And never have to breathe.

Life doesn't frighten me at all
Not at all
Not at all
Life doesn't frighten me at all.

Maya Angelou

Activity 4

At some time in our lives, particularly when we were very young, most of us have felt very frightened. Often such fears were associated with darkness, such as walking home after dark, a pitch black bedroom and unfamiliar shadows. Fears may also arise at other times and other places, such as when we are in high places, or confronted with spiders or snakes, for example.

continued

Activity 4 – *continued*

- With a friend, talk about occasions when you have felt really scared, then read Maya Angelou's poem. Talk about the fears in the poem and the way they are overcome.

Notice how the first two verses are constructed: two rhyming lines about the fears followed by the phrase 'Life doesn't frighten me at all.' This pattern is then repeated, after which, in verse three, the fears are banished in a series of short rhyming lines.

- Write your own poem in this pattern, using Maya Angelou's title and repeating it every few lines as she has done.

Serious Luv

Monday Morning

I really luv de girl dat's sitting next to me
I think she thinks like me and she's so cool,
I think dat we could live for ever happily
I want to marry her when I leave school.

She's de only one in school allowed to call me Ben
When she does Maths I luv de way she chews her pen,
When we are doing Art she's so artistic
In Biology she makes me heart beat so quick.

When we do Geography I go to paradise
She's helped me draw a map of Borneo twice!
Today she's going to help me to take me books home
So I am going to propose to her when we're alone.

The next day

I used to luv de girl dat's sitting next to me
But yesterday it all came to an end,
She said that I should take love more seriously
And now I think I really luv her friend.

Benjamin Zephaniah

Lizzie

When I was eleven
there was Lizzie.
I used to think this:

You don't care, Lizzie,
you say
that you're a ginger-nut
and you don't care.

I've noticed
that they try to soften you up

they say
you're clumsy
they say
you can't wear shorts

to school
but you say,
'I don't care,
I mean
how can I play football
in a skirt?'

Lizzie,
I'm afraid of saying
I think you're great

because, you see,
the teachers call you
tomboy.

I'm sorry
but I make out, as if
I agree with the teachers

and the other girls
wear bracelets
and I've noticed
they don't shout like you
or whistle,
and, you see,
the other boys
are always talking about

those girls
with the bracelets

So I do too.

So I know
that makes me a coward
but that's why I don't dare
to say you're great,

but I think it to myself
when you're there
but I don't say.

I just try to show
I like you
by laughing
and joking about
and pulling mad faces.

I'm sorry
but I don't suppose
you'll ever know...

Michael Rosen

154

Activity 5

The poems *Serious Luv* and *Lizzie* capture the mixed feelings that first love can bring.

- The poems are written from a boy's point of view and both mask their feelings with humour. Why is this?
- Would a girl try to attract a boy's attention in similar ways to the boys in these poems?
- Try writing your own poem on a similar theme.

My Sari

Saris hang on the washing line:
a rainbow in our neighbourhood.
This little orange one is mine,
it has a mango leaf design.
I wear it as a Rani* would.
It wraps around me like sunshine,
it ripples silky down my spine,
and I stand tall and feel so good.

*Indian queen/Rajah's wife

Debjani Chatterjee

People Ask

My father travelled from Ceylon
Island of cinnamon and rubies
To my mother's birthplace
In the heart of Yorkshire.

People ask
Where do you come from?
I say:
From more places
than you imagine
My father's memories
My mother's dreams
Mines of gems and coal
Mango sunsets over rhubarb fields

People ask
Which half of you is white?
I say:
There are no halves in me
Everything is whole
I am a myriad of mingling
Multicoloured stories
Whispering wisely down
through centuries

People ask
Where do you belong?
I say:
In the world
In my father's hopes
In my mother's songs
Most of all
In the place inside myself
Shining with its own futures.

Seni Seneviratne

'Ere She Said

'Ere, she said,
Her fag hanging out of her mouth,
Dropping both ash and H's.
'Ere, she said,
Was you born 'ere?
Only you speak very good English.
Where d'ya come from then?
Africa?

Only askin' cos what's 'er name comes from
    there
But she ain't your colouring,
She's darker, much darker
Than you.

And do ya eat food – like what we do?
Y'know, red meat and Yorkshire Pud?
Only what's 'er name says she don't.
She eats – what d'ya call 'em –
Balls of dough, fried like dumplings.

'Ere, she said. Listen to this.
I've bin wif out 'eat for five weeks,
Just bin on to the Council.
But the man said he couldn't unnerstan' me.
Didn't unnerstan' me accent.
Bleeding Asian weren't he!

Sorry...din't mean you.
I mean you're not like the rest of 'em.
Are you?

Gita Bedi

Activity 6

- Read the three poems.

- In *My Sari* and *People Ask*, what gives the poets their sense of self and pride?

- In her poem *'Ere She Said*, Gita Bedi is composed and sees the humour of the situation. What are the reasons for the confusion shown by the woman who questions her?

Brendon Gallacher

He was seven and I was six, my Brendon Gallacher,
He was Irish and I was Scottish, my Brendon Gallacher.
His father was in prison; he was a cat burglar.
My father was a communist party full-time worker.
He had six brothers and I had one, my Brendon Gallacher.

He would hold my hand and take me by the river
Where we'd talk all about his family being poor.
He'd get his mum out of Glasgow when he got older.
A wee holiday some place nice. Some place far.
I'd tell my mum about Brendon Gallacher

How his mum drank and his daddy was a cat burglar.
And she'd say 'Why not have him round to dinner?'
No, no, I'd say he's got big holes in his trousers.
I like meeting him by the burn in the open air.
Then one day after we'd been friends for two years,

One day when it was pouring and I was indoors,
My mum says to me, 'I was talking to Mrs Moir
Who lives next door to your Brendon Gallacher
Didn't you say his address was 24 Novar?
She says there are no Gallachers at 24 Novar

There never have been any Gallachers next door.'
And he died then, my Brendon Gallacher,
Flat out on my bedroom floor, his spiky hair,
His impish grin, his funny flapping ear.
O Brendon. O my Brendon Gallacher.

Jackie Kay

Activity 7

- Hear the poem *Brendan Gallacher* read aloud.
- What do we learn of Brendon and his character?
- Why do you think Jackie might have invented Brendon Gallacher?

Old Tongue

When I was eight, I was forced south.
Not long after, when I opened
my mouth, a strange thing happened.
I lost my Scottish accent.
Words fell off my tongue:
eedyit, dreich, wabbit, crabbit
stummer, teuchter, heidbanger,
so you are, so am ur, see you, see ma ma,
shut yer geggie or I'll gie you the malkie!

My own vowels started to stretch like my
    bones
and I turned my back on Scotland.
Words disappeared in the dead of night,
new words marched in: ghastly, awful,
quite dreadful, *scones* said like *stones.*
Pokey hats into ice cream cones.
Oh where did all my words go —
my old words, my lost words?
Did you ever feel sad when you lost a word,
did you ever try and call it back
like calling in the sea?
If I could have found my words wandering,
I swear I would have taken them in,
swallowed them whole, knocked them back.

Out in the English soil, my old words
buried themselves. It made my mother's
    blood boil.
I cried one day with the wrong sound in my
    mouth.
I wanted them back; I wanted my old accent
    back,
my old tongue. My dour soor Scottish
    tongue.
Sing-songy. I wanted to *gie it laldie.*

Jackie Kay

eedyit = idiot • *dreich* = dreary, wet, miserable • *wabbit* = tired, run down • *crabbit* = crabby, irritable • *stummer* = thick-witted • *teuchter* = a term of contempt used in Central Scotland for a Highlander • *heidbanger* = a wild, crazy person • *so am ur* = so am I • *geggie* = mouth • *gie you the malkie* = severely hurt someone • *soor* = sour • *gie it laldie* = give a good beating

Activity 8

- Hear the poem read aloud.
- What upset her most about losing her Scots words and finding she was using southern English ones instead?
- Is her language important to her identity? Is yours important to you? Why?

English Cousin Comes to Scotland

See when my English cousin comes,
it's so embarrassing so it is, so it is.
I have to explain everything
I mean Every Thing, so I do, so I do.
I told her, 'Know what happened to me?
I got skelped, because I screamed when a skelf
went into my pinky finger: OUCH, loud.
And am ma dropped her best bit of china.
It wis sore, so it wis, so it wis.
I was scunnert being skelped
when I wis already sore.
So I ran and ran, holding
my pinky, through the park,
over the burn, up the hill.
I was knackered and I fell
into the mud and went home
mocket and got skelped again.
So I locked myself in the cludgie
and cried, so I did, do I did,
pulling the long roll of paper
onto the floor. Like that dug Andrex.'
Whilst I'm saying this, my English cousin
has her mouth open. Glaikit.
Stupit. So she is, so she is.
I says, 'I'm going to have to learn you
what's what.' And at that the wee git
cheers up; the wee toffee nose says,
'Not learn you, teach you,' like she's
    scored.

Jackie Kay

Skelped = smacked • *skelf* = splinter • *pinky* = little finger • *scunnert* = annoyed • *mocket* = filthy, dirty • *cludgie* = toilet • *dug* = dog • *glaikit* = stupid, dazed-looking

Activity 9

- Hear the poem on page **161** read aloud.

- Why is her cousin 'glaikit'?

- What little triumph does the visiting cousin think she has scored?

- What does Jackie think of this?

- Do you or your family have any words that are used in your area but not generally in others? These are **dialect** words. Can you find different words that are used for 'left-handed', 'freckles', 'to brew tea', 'catching', or 'children'?

A Small Dragon

I've found a small dragon in the woodshed.
Think it must have come from deep inside a forest
because it's damp and green leaves
are still reflecting in its eyes.

I fed it on many things, tried grass,
the roots of stars, hazel-nut and dandelion,
but it stared up at me as if to say, I need
foods you can't provide.

It made its nest among the coal
not unlike a bird's but larger,
it is out of place here
and it is mosttimes silent.

If you believed in it I would come
hurrying to your house to let you share this wonder,
but I want instead to see
if you yourself will pass this way.

Brian Patten

Activity 10

- Read the poem *A Small Dragon*.

- Finding small dragons in the woodshed is not all that common in reality, so what does it suggest about the writer? What does he hope will happen? Who do you think the 'you yourself' of the last verse might be?

Street Boy

Just you look at me, man,
Stompin' down the street
My crombie stuffed with biceps
My boots is filled with feet.

Just you hark to me, man,
When they call us out
My head is full of silence
My mouth is full of shout.

Just you watch me move, man,
Steady like a clock
My heart is spaced on blue beat
My soul is stoned on rock.

Just you read my name, man,
Writ for all to see
The walls in red with stories
The streets is filled with me.

Gareth Owen

Unit 9
YOU

Most of the poems in this section are about the process of growing up from babyhood, through childhood, and into the teenage years. All of them are written by adults, many of them looking back on family memories.

Activity 1

- What do you remember about your earliest years?
  - Which of the class can go back the furthest with their memory?
  - Does one incident stand out clearly and sharply in your memory?
  - Are there any similarities in the things each of you remembers? Are they sad or happy or frightening?
  - Can you distinguish what you were told by your parents from what *you* actually recall?
- Focus upon one particular memory that is significant to you. Write down notes to capture the feelings, and form them into a poem which recalls the incident and why it stands out in your personal history.

On My First Sonne

Farewell, thou child of my right hand, and joy;
My sinne was too much hope of thee, lov'd boy
Seven yeeres tho' wert lent to me, and I thee pay,
Exacted by thy fate, on the just day.
O, could I loose all father, now. For why
Will man lament the state he should envie?
To have so soone scap'd worlds, and fleshes rage,
And, if no other miserie, yet age?
Rest in soft peace, and, ask'd, say here doth lye
Ben. Jonson his best piece of poetrie.
For whose sake, hence-forth, all his vowes be such,
As what he loves may never like too much.

Ben Jonson

On My First Daughter

Here lies, to each her parents' ruth *,   * sorrow, grief
Mary, the daughter of their youth;
Yet all heaven's gifts being heaven's due,
It makes the father less to rue *.   * grieve
At six months' end, she parted hence
With safety of her innocence;
Whose soul heaven's queen *, whose name she bears,   * Mary
In comfort of her mother's tears,
Hath placed amongst her virgin-train:
Where, while that severed doth remain,
This grave partakes the fleshly birth;
Which cover lightly, gentle earth!

Ben Jonson

Activity 2

On My First Sonne is an **elegy** for the poet's son who died aged 7 in 1603. The poem dates from a time, four centuries ago, when death in childhood was common and when faith in God was more widespread than it is today. *On My First Daughter* (Mary, who died aged just six months in 1593) is about the daughter born early in his marriage.

- Hear the poems read aloud. They are of a previous age and the language is sometimes difficult, but the feelings of grief are as raw today as they were when they were written.

- Think about the father's feelings: what comfort does he find in these deaths? What consolation does writing the poems offer him?

Morning Song

Love set you going like a fat gold watch.
The midwife slapped your footsoles, and your bald cry
Took its place among the elements.

Our voices echo, magnifying your arrival. New statue.
In a drafty museum, your nakedness
Shadows our safety. We stand round blankly as walls.

I'm no more your mother
Than the cloud that distils a mirror to reflect its own slow
Effacement at the wind's hand.

All night your moth-breath
Flickers among the flat pink roses. I wake to listen:
A far sea moves in my ear.

One cry, and I stumble from bed, cow-heavy and floral
In my Victorian nightgown.
Your mouth opens clean as a cat's. The window square

Whitens and swallows its dull stars. And now you try
Your handful of notes;
The clear vowels rise like balloons.

Sylvia Plath

Activity 3

Morning Song is about Sylvia Plath's sense of becoming a mother – the mixture of closeness, separateness, and responsibility for the new-born child.

- How do her conflicting feelings develop through the poem?
- There are several striking comparisons in the poem, both metaphors and similes. Identify them and describe the pictures they make in your mind's eye and the feelings they suggest.

Balloons

Since Christmas they have lived with us,
Guileless and clear,
Oval soul-animals,
Taking up half the space,
Moving and rubbing on the silk

Invisible air drifts,
Giving a shriek and pop
When attacked, then scooting to rest,
    barely trembling.
Yellow cathead, blue fish————
Such queer moons we live with

Instead of dead furniture!
Straw mats, white walls
And these travelling
Globes of thin air, red, green,
Delighting

The heart like wishes or free
Peacocks blessing
Old ground with a feather
Beaten in starry metals.
Your small

Brother is making
His balloon squeak like a cat.
Seeming to see
A funny pink world he might eat on the
    other side of it,
He bites,

Then sits
Back, fat jug
Contemplating a world clear as water.
A red
Shred in his little fist.

Sylvia Plath

165

Activity 4

- Read the poem and share the mother and child's pleasure in the simple happiness a room full of Christmas balloons can bring.

- As in *Morning Song* there are several striking images. Pick out any that appeal to you and share them.

Born Yesterday

Tightly-folded bud,
I have wished you something
None of the others would:
Not the usual stuff
About being beautiful,
Or running off a spring
Of innocence and love -
They will all wish you that,
And should it prove possible,
Well, you're a lucky girl.

But if it shouldn't, then
May you be ordinary;
Have, like other women,
An average of talents:
Not ugly, not good-looking,
Nothing uncustomary
To pull you off your balance,
That, unworkable itself,
Stops all the rest from working.
In fact, may you be dull -
If that is what a skilled,
Vigilant, flexible,
Unemphasised, enthralled
Catching of happiness is called.

Philip Larkin

Activity 5

The poem was written for Sally Amis, the daughter of the writer Kingsley Amis, at her birth.

- Read the poem and discuss just what it is the poet wishes for the new child.
- What does he say in the first ten lines about the traditional gifts that others would wish for her?
- What does he say in the next ten lines that he hopes for her if the usual gifts (beauty, innocence, love etc.) don't work out?

At Seven a Son

In cold weather on a
garden swing, his legs
in wellingtons rising over
the winter rose trees

he sits serenely
smiling like a Thai
his coat open, his gloves
sewn to the flapping sleeves

his thin knees working
with his arms
folded about the
metal struts

as he flies up
(his hair like long
black leaves) he
lies back freely

astonished in
sunshine as serious
as a stranger he is
a bird in his own thought.

Elaine Feinstein

A Child Half-Asleep

Stealthily parting the small-hours silence,
a hardly-embodied figment of his brain
comes down to sit with me
as I work late.
Flat-footed, as though his legs and feet
were still asleep.

On a stool,
staring into the fire,
his dummy dangling.

Fire ignites the small coals of his eyes;
it stares back through the holes
into his head, into the darkness.

I ask what woke him.

'A wolf dreamed me ,' he says.

Tony Connor

167

Activity 6

- Read the two poems, *A Child Half-Asleep* and *At Seven a Son*.

- In *A Child Half-Asleep*, why is the last line, 'A wolf dreamed me' and not, 'I had a nightmare about a wolf'?

- The first four sections of *At Seven a Son* describe the boy on the swing. What does the last section say?

Children's Song

We live in our own world,
A world that is too small
For you to stoop and enter
Even on hands and knees,
The adult subterfuge*.   *trick, excuse
And though you probe and pry
With analytic eye,
And eavesdrop all our talk
With an amused look,
You cannot find the centre
Where we dance, where we play,
Where life is still asleep
Under the closed flower,
Under the smooth shell
Of eggs in the cupped nest
That mock faded blue
Of your remoter heaven.

R.S. Thomas

Activity 7

- The phrase 'adult subterfuge' in line 5 refers to the behaviour of grown-ups pretending to be children by going down on their hands and knees to play with little ones. It is one of three things, mentioned in the first half of the poem, that adults do to try to enter the child's world. What are the other two?

- In the second half of the poem, what comparisons are used to suggest the child's world?

- What words in the last two lines suggest that adults have now lost touch with childhood and cannot really connect with it any more?

Sally

She was a dog-rose kind of girl:
Elusive, scattery as petals;
Scratchy sometimes, tripping you like briars.
She teased the boys
Turning this way and that, not to be tamed
Or taught any more than the wind.
Even in school the word 'ought' had no meaning
For Sally. On dull days
She'd sit quiet as a mole at her desk
Delving in thought.
But when the sun called
She was gone, running the blue day down
Till the warm hedgerows prickled the dusk
And moths flickered out.

Her mother scolded; Dad
Gave her the hazel switch,
Said her head was stuffed with feathers
And a starling tongue.
But they couldn't take the shine out of her,
Even when it rained
You felt the sun saved under the skin.
She'd a way of escape
Laughing at you from the bright end of a tunnel,
Leaving you in the dark.

Phoebe Hesketh

Activity 8

- Read the poem. Although the girl in the poem is a character from several generations ago, you may know someone like her (a dog-rose is a pretty, wild rose that flowers in hedges and usually has sharp thorns).

- How do you think the poet feels about Sally's behaviour?

Little Johnny's Final Letter

Mother,

I won't be home this evening, so
don't worry; don't hurry to report me missing.
Don't drain the canals to find me,
I've decided to stay alive, don't
search the woods, I'm not hiding,
simply gone to get myself classified.
Don't leave my Shreddies out,
I've done with security.
Don't circulate my photograph to society
I have disguised myself as a man
and am giving priority to obscurity.
It suits me fine;
I have taken off my short trousers
and put on long ones, and
now am going out into the city, so
don't worry; don't hurry to report me missing.

I've rented a room without any curtains
and sit behind the windows growing cold,
heard your plea on the radio this morning,
you sounded sad and strangely old....

Brian Patten

Activity 9

The poem is a series of pleas from teenager Johnny to his mother to don't do this or that in order for her to find him!

- What does this suggest about his feelings of running away from home?

- How do you sense the poet feels about the boy?

Oxygen

I am the very air
you breathe
Your first
and last
breath

I welcomed you
at birth
Shall bid farewell
at death

I am the Kiss of Life
its ebb and flow
With your last grasp
You will call my name:
'o o o o o o o'

Roger McGough

Spell of the Air

I am the impulse of all whispers, I
    Am the place for a rush of birds,
I am the whole intention of the sky
    And the place for coining words.

I am your life breathing in and out,
    I set your senses free,
I sort the truth from complicated doubt,
    I am necessity.

Elizabeth Jennings

171

Unit 10

POEMS AND PAINTINGS

Brueghel

Peter Brueghel; Landscape With The Fall Of Icarus, c.1555

In Greek myth, Icarus was the son of Daedalus, a brilliant inventor, who had been imprisoned on the island of Crete by King Minos. Father and son escaped using wings made by Daedalus from wax and feathers. Ignoring his father's warnings, the boy flew towards the sun, melting the wax in his wings and hurtling to the sea and a watery death.

Activity 1

- Look carefully at the painting. How many people can you see? What is each one doing? Where is each one looking?

- What is the most important thing happening in the picture? Is it the man ploughing? The ship sailing away or something else?

Three quite different poets wrote three quite different poems about this picture.

Activity 2

- Hear the poem by William Carlos Williams read aloud.

- How does the poem reflect the atmosphere of the painting?

(Think about the punctuation and about why the writer uses certain words and phrases. Answering the questions alongside the poem should help you).

Landscape with the Fall of Icarus

According to Brueghel
when Icarus fell
it was spring

a farmer was ploughing
his field
the whole pageantry

of the year was
awake tingling
near

1 What does this way of putting it, 'According to Breughel,' suggest?

2 What ideas does 'it was spring' suggest?

3 'Awake tingling' suggests the scene is full of life. What does this contrast with?

the edge of the sea
concerned
with itself

sweating in the sun
that melted
the wings' wax

unsignificantly
off the coast
there was

4 How does the word 'unsignificantly' echo
what is happening in the painting?

a splash quite unnoticed
this was
Icarus drowning.

5 What about the word 'unnoticed'?
6 What is the tone. The last two lines?
Why does the poet take this tone?

William Carlos Williams

In contrast to the understated way in which William Carlos Williams portrays Icarus' fall and death, the poet Gareth Owen chooses a first person narrative. Icarus phones his father from his mobile as he plummets earthwards.

Activity 3

- Read the poem and then answer the questions alongside it.

Icarus by Mobile

Daddy, Daddy, is that you?
Listen I don't have much time OK.
But I wanted to say, right
It's back to the drawing board Daddy
The whole contraption is a no no.
The wings?
No, the wings worked fine
Couldn't fault the wings in any way
The wings were ace

1 What concerns Icarus (and his father) most
during this first part of the call?

And your calculations on the stresses
Re wind and feathers
Spot on!
Likewise the pinion tolerances
And remember that flap factor
That gave us both such sleepless nights
Let me tell you
Those flaps worked like a dream.
But Daddy
Oh Daddy
How could you forget the sun!
I don't have much time
So listen OK.
We're talking equations here
Just let me spell it out for you:
Solar heat + bees wax + ambition =
Total Meltdown and I mean total
Which equals, to put it simply,
Your boy Icarus is on collision course
With something called the Earth.
Daddy I don't have much time
Let me give the co-ordinates
For the pick-up
OK stretch of headland and a bay
Visibility good, outlook calm
And hey
Am I lucky
Or am I lucky!
There's a galleon anchored near the shore
Looks like Icarus
Is in for an early pick up this fine morning.
And over there some poor old farmer's
Ploughing through a field of stones
And here's an old boy with a fishing pole
and
Listen Daddy
Would you believe
Some guy just out of frame
Is painting the whole thing.
And now I'm waving Daddy, waving

2 Whose ambition is he referring to?

175

3 What is Icarus' mood as he gives the coordinates for the pick-up?

4 Who would the 'guy painting' be? Where does the perspective of the painting suggest the painter is positioned?

Any minute now they'll look up and
So listen Daddy I don't have much time
I'm going to start screaming soon OK.
Can you still hear me?
I don't have much
Daddy, I just wanted to ask
You know
About my mum
Was she
Listen Daddy
I don't have much time
I

5 Will the farmer, fisherman, sailors and shepherd look up?

6 Icarus' mother was a slave and mistress of King Minos who had imprisoned Icarus and his father.

What does the unexpected question about her at the end suggest about Icarus' state of mind now as opposed to just a few seconds earlier?

Gareth Owen

The poet W. H. Auden also wrote about Brueghel's *Icarus*. He links it to other paintings by great artists of the past, the Old Masters, and the way in which they depicted suffering in their paintings.

Musée des Beaux Arts*   *Fine Art Museum

About suffering they were never wrong,
The Old Masters: how well they understood
Its human position; how it takes place
While someone else is eating or opening a window or just walking dully along;
How, when the aged are reverently, passionately waiting
For the miraculous birth, there always must be
Children who do not specially want it to happen, skating
On a pond at the edge of the wood:
They never forgot
That even the dreadful martyrdom must run its course
Anyhow in a corner, some untidy spot
Where the dogs go on with their doggy life and the torturer's horse
Scratches its innocent behind on a tree.

In Brueghel's *Icarus*, for instance: how everything turns away
Quite leisurely from the disaster; the ploughman may
Have heard the splash, the forsaken cry,
But for him it was not an important failure; the sun shone
As it had to on the white legs disappearing into the green
Water; and the expensive delicate ship that must have seen
Something amazing, a boy falling out of the sky,
Had somewhere to get to and sailed calmly on.

W.H. Auden

Activity 4

- Read the poem on page **176**.

- Who were The Old Masters? What is it that they understood about the nature of suffering?

- What kind of painting does he have in mind when he writes of 'the dreadful martyrdom'?

- How does the poem relate to us and our world? You might consider that as you read the poem, now, today, people are suffering and dying of starvation or AIDS, being tortured, and killed in wars.

Magritte

René Magritte, *Time Transfixed, 1939*, The Art Institute of Chicago

Activity 5

Look carefully at the painting on page **177** and write down any ideas, questions or associations that it raises in your mind however strange or absurd they may appear to be.

Activity 6

- With a friend, discuss your first thoughts.
- What is it about the scale of the fireplace and the engine that first surprises you?
- What kind of room is it?
- How does the train engine contrast with the room?
- Why do you think Magritte gave the painting the title *Time Transfixed?*

Time Transfixed

Time will stand still
When the lift in the multi storey
Rockets through the roof
And takes its place
Motionless amongst a million stars.

Time will stand still
When the cold March wind
Is weary of whistling
And suddenly stops –
A solid chunk of air.

Time will stand still
When a train hits the buffers,
Bursts through (to the amazement of
    pigeons)
And stands, its smoke frozen,
In my empty fireplace.

Heather Harvey

Time Transfixed *by René Magritte*

In the Thinking Room
at Childhood Hall,
the brown clock ticks
with the sound of the kiss
that my Grandma makes
against my cheek
again and again
when we first meet
after a week
of all the hours
that the brown clock's tick
has kissed away
today, to-
morrow, yesterday

are all the same
to the plum steam-train
that I sometimes hear
in the Thinking Room
at Childhood Hall –
it has no passengers at all,
till I grow old enough
and tall
to climb aboard
the plum steam-train
and blow a kiss
as I chuff away to to-
morrow, yesterday, today.

Carol Ann Duffy

Activity 7

- Read the two poems.

- In Heather Harvey's poem, what are the two other dream-like images she suggests for time standing still?

- In Carol Ann Duffy's poem, what does the tick of the clock remind her of at first? What does this make her think about time?

- What will happen when Carol Ann Duffy climbs aboard the train?

Activity 8

- Read Carole Satyamurti's poem, *Leaving Present*, first with the questions covered so as not to distract you. Then answer the questions alongside.

Leaving Present

(Magritte's *Time Transfixed*)

The retirement clock: he's done his time,
now's the time for the time of his life,
for all the time in the world.
He places the clock where it can see him.

Time has always come in blocks. Now
it floods the landscape of his days,
runs through his fingers.
His thoughts dissolve in it like Disprin.

Time keeping's as unnecessary as he is.
He'd like to jump on a train to anywhere
but this blank-faced body-guard
is watching, its clipped, dry voice

foretelling mean time,
injury time, time out of mind,
the moment when his time
is up, is up, is up.

Carole Satyamurti

1 There are two possible meanings to the title 'Leaving Present'. What are they?

2 'he's done his time'; 'the time of his life'; 'all the time in the world.'
What does each of these three phrases mean? What mood do they suggest at first?
What other possible meanings could they have?

3 How does he feel now in verse 3 compared with his feelings in verse1?

4 'mean time'; 'injury time'; 'time out of mind.'
Each of these three phrases suggests two meanings. What do they foretell?

Activity 9

- Write your own poem about the painting. If you are looking for a place to start, you could think about what might have happened just before or just after the moment of the painting. You could write your poem from the point of view of the engine driver or someone sitting in the room. Or, you could use Heather Harvey's verses as a model for your own poem and pattern your verses in the same way that she has:

Time will stand still

When ....

....

And..................

....

You could build a class poem of several verses in this way.

Activity 10

A surreal painting like *Time Transfixed* puts ordinary things together in unexpected, dream-like ways.

- Can you think of other places where this surreal style is used? Music videos, television and magazine adverts, book jackets, computer games and CD inserts should all provide examples.

- Create your own surreal scene. You could imagine, illustrate or write about a dream landscape or a dream room. You might like to use a 'surrealist image generator' to get you started. Just link the ideas below randomly together (add your own, if you like):

Imagine:

a computer	crawling with ants	on a beach
a tree	on fire	in a wardrobe
a cloud	balanced on a rock	in a coffin
a supermarket trolley	in mid-air	under a full moon

Arcimboldo

Spring

Summer

Autumn

Winter

Activity 11

- Make a list of all the plants, flowers, fruit and vegetables you recognise in each of these four paintings and say which part of the body they represent. Arrange your notes according to season like this:

Spring

cheeks: roses

shoulder: cabbage

Summer

eye-ball: cherry

cheek: peach

- Consider how the colours change from season to season. What else changes as the year progresses?

Activity 12

- Read Julie O'Callaghan's two poems and notice how she puts into words many of the items that make up the heads. Using your own lists, write the poems about summer and autumn in the same style.

Spring

She is a flower arrangement
hearing through a peony ear
chewing with lily-of-the-valley teeth

Dew falls on her carnation cheek,
sparkles in violet eyes.
She talks with rosebud lips.

Julie O'Callaghan

Winter

He looks out of a crack in the bark:
a white mushroom mouth,
a bare head of stubs, vines and roots

waiting for warmth.
The moss on his neck is dead
and yellow — an old stubble.

He is a grey ghost
hiding in the forest —warty nose
more pale than cauliflower ear.

Julie O'Callaghan

Miro

Joan Miro, *Mural*, March 20, 1961

Activity 13

- Look at Miro's painting. It is a mural or wall-painting and it's big (about four metres long and over one metre high). With a friend, discuss what the shapes and colours suggest to you. Is it *of* anything? Is it *about* anything? Or is it just an experience? If it is an experience, is it one to be enjoyed? One to worry about? Something else?

I Would Like to be a Dot in a Painting by Miro

I would like to be a dot in a painting by Miro.

Barely distinguishable from other dots,
it's true, but quite uniquely placed.
And from my dark centre

I'd survey the beauty of the linescape
and wonder —would it be worthwhile
to roll myself towards the lemon stripe,

Centrally poised, and push my curves
against its edge, to get myself
a little extra attention?

But it's fine where I am.
I'll never make out what's going on
around me, and that's the joy of it.

The fact that I'm not a perfect circle
makes me more interesting in this world.
People will stare forever—

Even the most unemotional get excited.
So here I am, on the edge of animation,
a dream, a dance, a fantastic construction,

A child's adventure.
And nothing in this tawny sky
can get too close, or move too far away.

Moniza Alvi

Activity 14

- Read the poem by Moniza Alvi.

- The dot tells us quite a lot about itself. What sort of character would you say it has?

- Write your own brief comment on the poem. You only need write just one sentence to sum up what the poem suggests to you.

Activity 15

- Now read and discuss the following reactions to the poem:

  "I think Moniza is trying to get across the fact that not everyone is noticed. It's like judging a book by its cover. In the line 'People will stare forever', she means that finally she has become important." (Janine, aged 13)

  "It seems that the dot fancies the lemon stripe and it wants to be like the artist and survey the beauty of the linescape." (Tam, aged 13)

Activity 16

- Study the painting again and find a detail that appeals to you. Write your own poem, beginning:

  'I would like to be a...in a painting by Miro.'

  Insert the detail you have chosen in this first line and see where your imagination can lead you.

PART

TEN

POETS

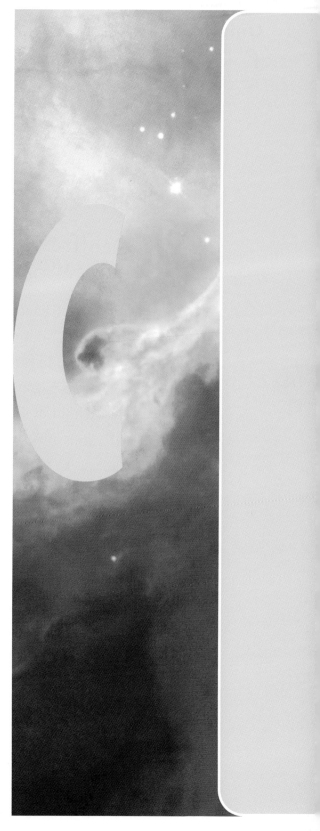

Unit 1
CHAUCER

Geoffrey Chaucer
c.1343 – 1400

Geoffrey Chaucer was the son of a rich London wine merchant. In his early teens he became a pageboy in the household of one of Edward II's sons and, during the rest of his life, he was to work as a courtier, civil servant and diplomat for three successive kings: Edward III, Richard II and Henry IV.

Chaucer had a busy and varied life; he travelled abroad as a soldier, he became a JP and a Knight of the Shire (Member of Parliament) and held many important posts, including controller of customs for the wool trade. These experiences gave him the opportunity to meet all sorts of different people and he used this knowledge in his most famous work, *The Canterbury Tales*, which is the story of a group of pilgrims on their way to Canterbury.

The Canterbury Tales

The Canterbury Tales is a collection of 24 stories of different kinds told by members of a company of Pilgrims on a journey one Spring from the Tabard Inn in Southwark, South London to the shrine of Thomas à Becket at Canterbury in Kent.

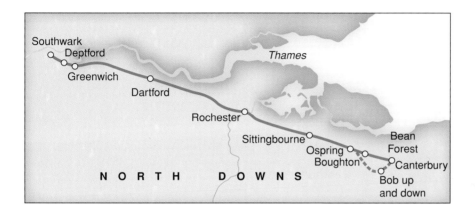

One of the main attractions of *The Canterbury Tales* is the variety of tellers as well as of their stories. There is a wide range of characters of whom we introduce you to just three – the Miller, the Wife of Bath and the Pardoner. The two men are rogues and the Wife of Bath is a very worldly women who tells us with some relish that she has had five husbands. They, like their companions, tell stories appropriate to their personality and station in life. In the selections that follow, there are the opening and closing passages of 'The General Prologue' which set up the story-telling plan, together with the pen-portraits of these three pilgrims.

Speaking the lines

Remember – these are stories in verse which were supposed to be spoken aloud to entertain the company. So, why not have a go yourself at speaking Chaucer?

Here are some rules to get you started:

Vowel sounds

i) the final -e or -es of words is spoken as an extra syllable.

ii) doubling the vowel -ee, -oo, -aa usually lengthens the sound.

iii) -a is pronounced flat, as in Northern English.

Consonant sounds   all consonants are pronounced, e.g.

i) 'Knyght' – the initial 'k' plus 'gh' as in 'loch', and the final 't'.

ii) 'folk' – pronounce the 'l'

iii) 'ion' or 'ious' – pronounce in two syllables.

Don't be afraid of making mistakes. Once you get used to the sounds and rhythm of the lines, you will find that the characters and stories are more colourful in Chaucer's language than in the modern version alongside. We have provided this recent translation to help you with difficult words and to give continuity to the descriptions, but don't let it stop you speaking Chaucer's lines. To read that the Miller had a tuft of hairs on a wart on the end of his nose sounds rather tame beside:

> 'Upon the cop right of his nose he hade
> A werte, and theron stood a toft of herys,
> Reed as the brustles of a sowes erys…'

From: The General Prologue

I The Introduction

The Prologue begins with an 18-line sentence in praise of Spring and an explanation of the company gathered at the Tabard Inn.

Prologue

Whan that Aprill with his shoures soote
The droghte of March hath perced to the roote,
And bathed every veyne in swich licour
Of which vertu engendred is the flour;
Whan Zephirus eek with his sweete breeth
Inspired hath in every holt and heeth
The tendre croppes, and the yonge sonne
Hath in the Ram his halve cours yronne,
And smale foweles maken melodye,
That slepen al the nyght with open ye
(So priketh hem nature in hir corages);
Thanne longen folk to goon on pilgrimages,
And palmeres for to seken straunge strondes,
To ferne halwes, kowthe in sondry londes;
And specially from every shires ende
Of Engelond to Caunterbury they wende,
The hooly blisful martir for to seke,
That hem hath holpen whan that they were seeke.
   Bifil that in that seson on a day,
In Southwerk at the Tabard as I lay
Redy to wenden on my pilgrymage
To Caunterbury with ful devout corage,
At nyght was come into that hostelrye
Wel nyne and twenty in a compaignye,
Of sondry folk, by aventure yfalle
In felaweshipe, and pilgrimes were they alle,
That toward Caunterbury wolden ryde.
The chambres and the stables weren wyde,
And wel we weren esed atte beste.
And shortly, whan the sonne was to reste,
So hadde I spoken with hem everichon
That I was of hir felaweship anon,
And made forward erly for to rise,
To take oure wey there as I yow devyse.

Translation

When the sweet showers of April have pierced
The drought of March, and pierced it to the root,
And every vein is bathed in that moisture
Whose quickening force will engender the flower;
And when the west wind too with its sweet breath
Has given life in every wood and field
To tender shoots, and when the struggling sun
Has run his half-course in Aries, the Ram[1],
And when small birds are making melodies,
That sleep all the night long with open eyes,
(Nature so prompts them, and encourages);
Then people long to go on pilgrimages,
And palmers[2] to take ship for foreign shores,
And distant shrines, famous in different lands;
And most especially, from all the shires
Of England, to Canterbury they come
The holy blessed martyr[3] there to seek,
Who gave his help to them when they were sick.
   It happened at this season, that one day
In Southwark at the Tabard where I stayed
Ready to set out on my pilgrimage
To Canterbury, and pay devout homage,
There came at nightfall to the hostelry
Some nine-and-twenty in a company,
Folk of all kinds, met in accidental
Companionship, for they were pilgrims all;
It was to Canterbury that they rode.
The bedrooms and the stables were good-sized,
The comforts offered us were of the best.
And by the time the sun had gone to rest
I'd talked with everyone, and soon became
One of their company, and promised them
To rise at dawn next day to take the road
For the journey I am telling you about.

[1] first sign of the Zodiac
[2] pilgrims who had visited Jerusalem
[3] St Thomas à Becket

2 Three characters

The Miller

The MILLERE was a stout carl for the nones;
Ful byg he was of brawn, and eek of bones.
That proved wel, for over al ther he cam,
At wrastlynge he wolde have alwey the ram.
He was short-sholdred, brood, a thikke knarre;
Ther was no dore that he nolde heve of harre,
Or breke it at a rennyng with his heed.
His berd as any sowe or fox was reed,
And therto brood, as thought it were a spade.
Upon the cop right of his nose he hade
A werte, and theron stood a toft of herys,
Reed as the brustles of a sowes erys;
His nosethirles blake were and wyde.
A swerd and bokeler bar he by his syde.
His mouth as greet was as a greet forneys.
He was a janglere and a goliardeys.
And that was moost of synne and harlotries.
Wel koude he stelen corn and tollen thries;
And yet he hadde a thombe of gold, pardee.
A whit cote and a blew hood wered he.
A baggepipe wel koude he blowe and sowne,
And therwithal he broghte us out of towne.

Translation

The miller was a burly fellow—brawn
And muscle, big of bones as well as strong
As was well seen—he always won the ram
At wrestling-matches up and down the land.
He was barrel-chested, rugged and thickset,
And would heave off its hinges any door
Or break it running at it with his head.
His beard was red as any fox or sow,
And wide at that, as though it were a spade.
And on his nose, right on its tip, he had
A wart, upon which stood a tuft of hairs
Red as the bristles are in a sow's ear.
Black were his nostrils; black and squat and wide.
He bore a sword and buckler by his side.
His big mouth was as big as a furnace.
A loudmouth and a teller of blue stories
(Most of them vicious or scurrilous),
Well versed in stealing corn and trebling dues,
He had a golden thumb—by God he had!
A white coat he had on, and a blue hood.
He played the bagpipes well, and blew a tune,
And to its music brought us out of town.

The Miller   The Wife of Bath   The Pardoner

The Wife of Bath

A good WIF was ther of biside BATHE,
But she was somdel deef, and that was scathe.
Of clooth-makyng she hadde swich an haunt,
She passed hem of Ypres and of Gaunt.
In al the parisshe wif ne was ther noon
That to the offrynge bifore hire sholde goon;
And if ther dide, certeyn so wrooth was she,
That she was out of alle charitee.
Hir coverchiefs ful fyne weren of ground;
I dorste swere they weyeden ten pound
That on a Sonday weren upon hir heed.
Hir hosen weren of fyn scarlet reed,
Ful streite yteyd, and shoes ful moyste and newe.
Boold was hir face, and fair, and reed of hewe.
She was a worthy womman al hir lyve:
Housbondes at chirche dore she hadde fyve,
Withouten oother compaignye in youthe,—
But therof nedeth nat to speke as nowthe.
And thries hadde she been at Jerusalem;
She hadde passed many a straunge strem;
At Rome she hadde been, and at Boloigne,
In Galice at Seint-Jame, and at Coloigne.
She koude muchel of wandrynge by the weye.
Gat-tothed was she, soothly for to seye.
Upon an amblere esily she sat,
Ywympled wel, and on hir heed an hat
As brood as is a bokeler or a targe;
A foot-mantel aboute hir hipes large,
And on hir feet a paire of spores sharpe.
In felawshipe wel koude she laughe and carpe.
Of remedies of love she knew per chaunce,
For she koude of that art the olde daunce.

Translation

There was a business woman, from near Bath,
But, more's the pity, she was a bit deaf;
So skilled a clothmaker, that she outdistanced
Even the weavers of Ypres and Ghent.
In the whole parish there was not a woman
Who dared precede her at the almsgiving,
And if there did, so furious was she,
That she was put out of all charity.
Her headkerchiefs were of the finest weave,
Ten pounds and more they weighed, I do believe,
Those that she wore on Sundays on her head.
Her stockings were of finest scarlet red,
Very tightly laced; shoes pliable and new.
Bold was her face, and handsome; florid too.
She had been respectable all her life,
And five times married, that's to say in church,
Not counting other loves she'd had in youth,
Of whom, just now, there is no need to speak.
And she had thrice been to Jerusalem;
Had wandered over many a foreign stream;
And she had been at Rome, and at Boulogne,
St James of Compostella, and at Cologne;
She knew all about wandering – and straying:
For she was gap-toothed, if you take my meaning[1].
Comfortably on an ambling horse she sat,
Well-wimpled, wearing on her head a hat
That might have been a shield in size and shape;
A riding-skirt round her enormous hips,
Also a pair of sharp spurs on her feet.
In company, how she could laugh and joke!
No doubt she knew of all the cures for love,
For at that game she was a past mistress.

[1] a sign of sensuality

The Pardoner

This PARDONER hadde heer as yelow as wex,
But smothe it heeng as dooth a strike of flex;
By ounces henge his lokkes that he hadde,
And therwith he his shuldres overspradde;
But thynne it lay, by colpons oon and oon.
But hood, for jolitee, wered he noon,
For it was trussed up in his walet.
Hym thoughte he rood al of the newe jet;
Dischevelee, save his cappe, he rood al bare.
Swiche glarynge eyen hadde he as an hare.
A vernycle hadde he sowed upon his cappe.
His walet lay biforn hym in his lappe,
Bretful of pardoun, comen from Rome al hoot.
A voys he hadde as smal as hath a goot.
No berd hadde he, ne nevere sholde have;
As smothe it was as it were late shave.
I trowe he were a geldyng or a mare.
But of his craft, fro Berwyk into Ware,
Ne was ther swich another pardoner.
For in his male he hadde a pilwe-beer,
Which that he seyde was Oure Lady veyl;
He seyde he hadde a gobet of the seyl
That Seint Peter hadde, whan that he wente
Upon the see, til Jhesu Crist hym hente.
He hadde a croys of latoun ful of stones,
And in a glas he hadde pigges bones.
But with thise relikes, whan that he fond
A povre person dwellynge upon londe,
Upon a day he gat hym moore moneye
Than that the person gat in monthes tweye;
And thus, with feyned flaterye and japes,
He made the person and the peple his apes.
But trewely to tellen atte laste,
He was in chirche a noble ecclesiaste.
Wel koude he rede a lessoun or a storie,
But alderbest he song an offertorie;
For wel he wiste, whan that song was songe,
He moste preche and wel affile his tonge
To wynne silver, as he ful wel koude;
Therefore he song the murierly and loude.

Translation

This pardon-seller's hair was yellow as wax,
And sleekly-hanging, like a hank of flax.
In meagre clusters hung what hair he had;
Over his shoulders a few strands were spread,
But they lay thin, in rat's tails, one by one.
As for a hood, for comfort he wore none,
For it was stowed away in his knapsack.
Save for a cap, he rode with head all bare,
Hair loose; he thought it was the *dernier cri*.
He had big bulging eyes, just like a hare.
He'd sewn a veronica[1] on his cap.
His knapsack lay before him, on his lap.
Chockful of pardons, all come hot from Rome.
His voice was like a goat's, plaintive and thin.
He had no beard, nor was he like to have;
Smooth was his face, as if he had just shaved.
I took him for a gelding or a mare.
As for his trade, from Berwick down to Ware
You'd not find such another pardon-seller.
For in his bag he had a pillowcase
Which had been, so he said, Our Lady's veil;
He said he had a snippet of the sail
St Peter had, that time he walked upon
The sea, and Jesus Christ caught hold of him.
And he'd a brass cross, set with pebble-stones,
And a glass reliquary of pigs' bones.
But with these relics, when he came upon
Some poor up-country priest or backwoods parson,
In just one day he'd pick up far more money
Than any parish priest was like to see
In two whole months. With double-talk and tricks
He made the people and the priest his dupes.
But to speak the truth and do the fellow justice,
In church he made a splendid ecclesiastic.
He'd read a lesson, or saint's history,
But best of all he sang the offertory:
For, knowing well that when the hymn was sung,
He'd have to preach and polish and smooth his tongue
To raise—as only he knew how—the wind,
The louder and the merrier he would sing.

[1] a copy of the handkerchief of St Veronica

194

3 The story-telling plan

At the end of the Prologue, Chaucer as one of the company, explains his role as the story-teller of this Pilgrimage and covers himself from any criticism that might come his way because of the stories he tells and the language he uses.

Now have I toold you soothly, in a clause,
Th'estaat, th'array, the nombre and eek the cause
Why that assembled was this compaignye
In Southwerk at this gentil hostelrye
That highte the Tabard, faste by the Belle.
But now is tyme to yow for to telle
How that we baren us that ilke nyght,
Whan we were in that hostelrie alyght;
And after wol I telle of our viage
And al the remenaunt of our pilgrimage.
But first I pray yow, of youre curteisye,
That ye n'arette it nat my vileynye,
Thogh that I pleynly speke in this mateere,
To telle yow hir wordes and hir cheere,
Ne thogh I speke hir wordes proprely.
For this ye knowen al so wel as I,
Whoso shal telle a tale after a man,
He moot reherce as ny as evere he kan
Everich a word, if it be in his charge,
Al speke he never so rudeliche and large,
Or ellis he moot telle his tale untrewe,
Or feyne thyng, or fynde wordes newe.

And now I've told you truly and concisely
The rank, and dress, and number of us all,
And why we gathered in a company
In Southwark, at that noble hostelry
Known as the Tabard, that's hard by the Bell.
But now the time has come for me to tell
What passed among us, what was said and done
That night of our arrival at the inn;
And afterwards I'll tell you how we journeyed,
And all the remainder of our pilgrimage.
But first I beg you, not to put it down
To my ill-breeding, if my speech be plain
When telling what they looked like, what they said,
Or if I use the exact words they used.
For, as you all must know as well as I,
To tell a tale told by another man
You must repeat as nearly as you can
Each word, if that's the task you've undertaken,
However coarse or broad his language is;
Or, in the telling, you'll have to distort it
Or make things up, or find new words for it.
You can't hold back, even if he's your brother:
Whatever word is used, you must use also.

Unit 2

WILLIAM SHAKESPEARE

William Shakespeare

1564 – 1616

Very little is known of Shakespeare's early life except that he was born in Stratford-upon-Avon and probably attended the local grammar school. He married Ann Hathaway in 1582, when he was only 18, and they had three children: Susanna, Judith and Hamnet. Hamnet died when he was just 11. By 1592, Shakespeare was in London, acting with a theatre company, composing poetry and starting to write the plays that were to make him the world's most famous playwright.

Shakespeare wrote 38 plays, 154 sonnets and many other poems. His plays have been translated into every major language and are still performed all over the world.

Shakespeare's plays are mostly written in **blank verse** (unrhymed verse, but with a basic five-beat rhythm — as when you repeat the word 'again' five times), but they also contain passages of prose, chants and many songs. In this selection you will find many different forms, from a chant written in couplets to three complicated **sonnets** on aspects of love.

The two opening pieces are in blank verse. The first describes the pattern of human life through the famous extended metaphor of the stage on which the 'seven ages of man' are played out. The second is spoken by Queen Gertrude in *Hamlet*, in which Shakespeare gives us a word-painting of the death of Ophelia. This poetry has inspired dozens of actual paintings, of which the one by Millais is the most famous.

Then there are four songs from various plays. 'Full Fathom Five' is sung by Ariel, a magical spirit in *The Tempest*. The two love songs, sung by Feste, the clown in *Twelfth Night*, are in different moods: one describes love as something to be accepted and enjoyed when it presents itself; the other is a sad song of a love that is not returned. 'Now the hungry lion roars' is one of many songs sung by Puck, the mischievous spirit who serves King Oberon in *A Midsummer Night's Dream*. Finally, we have also included the well-known 'Witches' Chant' from *Macbeth* for you to rehearse and perform.

The last three poems are taken from Shakespeare's sequence of 154 sonnets, first published in 1609. The sonnet is traditionally the form used in love poetry; and a common theme concerns the effects of time on love, as can be seen in different ways in these three poems. In Number 12, 'Time's scythe' not only destroys the beauty of the natural world, it finally cuts down human life. In Number 106, Time is a figure for past history chronicled in accounts of knights and their ladies from earlier centuries. In Number 116, Time is the irresistible force for change in Nature which only a perfect, true and lasting love can overcome.

197

Blank Verse

All the world's a stage…

This famous speech is delivered by Jacques, a melancholy, brooding character who watches the action of the play as an outsider and commentator, but has little effect upon events.

All the world's a stage,
And all the men and women merely players;
They have their exits and their entrances;
And one man in his time plays many parts,
His acts being seven ages. At first the infant,
Mewling* and puking in the nurse's arms;   *crying feebly

Then the whining school-boy, with his satchel
And shining morning face, creeping like snail
Unwillingly to school. And then the lover,
Sighing like furnace, with a woeful ballad
Made to his mistress' eyebrow. Then a soldier,
Full of strange oaths, and bearded like the pard,*   *leopard, panther
Jealous in honour, sudden and quick in quarrel,
Seeking the bubble reputation
Even in the cannon's mouth. And then the justice,
In fair round belly with good capon* lin'd,   *male fowl ('capon justices' were
With eyes severe and beard of formal cut,   magistrates bribed by gifts of capons)
Full of wise saws and modern instances;
And so he plays his part. The sixth age shifts
Into the lean and slipper'd pantaloon,*   *feeble old man
With spectacles on nose and pouch on side;
His youthful hose, well sav'd, a world too wide
For his shrunk shank; and his big manly voice,
Turning again toward childish treble, pipes
And whistles in his sound. Last scene of all,
That ends this strange eventful history,
Is second childishness and mere oblivion;
Sans* teeth, sans eyes, sans taste, sans everything.   *without

As You Like It, Act 2, Scene 7, lines 139–166

The Death of Ophelia

Ophelia was the abandoned love of Prince Hamlet. In a deranged state of mind, she decked herself with flowers and drowned herself in a stream. Here is the Queen's description of what happened:

                                             *weeping willow tree associated
There is a willow* grows aslant a brook,   with forsaken love
That shows his hoar* leaves in the glassy stream;   *silvery grey
There with fantastic garlands did she come
Of crow-flowers, nettles, daisies, and long purples
That liberal* shepherds give a grosser* name,   *free-spoken   *more vulgar
But our cold* maids do dead men's fingers call them: *chaste
There, on the pendent boughs her coronet* weeds   *garland of wild flowers
Clambering to hang, an envious sliver* broke;   *spiteful small branch
When down her weedy trophies and herself
Fell in the weeping brook. Her clothes spread wide;

And, mermaid-like, awhile they bore her up:
Which time she chanted snatches of old tunes;
As one incapable* of her own distress,
Or like a creature native* and indued
Unto that element: but long it could not be
Till that* her garments, heavy with their drink,
Pull'd the poor wretch from her melodious lay*
To muddy death.

*unaware
*belonging to and able to live in water
*before
*song

Hamlet, Act 4, Scene 7

Sir John Everett Millais, *Ophelia*, 1851–52, The Tate Gallery (London)

199

Songs

Now the Hungry Lion Roars

Now the hungry lion roars,
   And the wolf behowls the moon;
Whilst the heavy ploughman snores,
   All with weary task fordone.
Now the wasted brands* do glow,   *dying embers of the fire
   Whilst the screech-owl, screeching loud,
Puts the wretch that lies in woe
   In remembrance of a shroud.
Now it is the time of night
   That the graves, all gaping wide,
Every one lets forth his sprite,
   In the church-way paths to glide:
And we fairies, that do run
   By the triple Hecate's* team,   *the moon's (called Diana on earth,
From the presence of the sun,   Phoebe in the sky, Hecate in the nether
   Following darkness like a dream,   world = three names)
Now are frolic*: not a mouse   *merry, frolicsome
   Shall disturb this hallow'd house:
I am sent with broom before,
   To sweep the dust behind the door.

A Midsummer Night's Dream, Act 5, Scene 1

Come Away, Come Away, Death

Come away, come away, death,
   And in sad cypress* let me be laid;   *coffin of cypress wood, strewn with
Fly away, fly away, breath;   cypress branches. Symbolic of
   I am slain by a fair cruel maid.   mourning
My shroud of white, stuck all with yew,
   O, prepare it!
My part of death, no one so true
   Did share it.
Not a flower, not a flower sweet
   On my black coffin let there be strown;
Not a friend, not a friend greet
   My poor corse*, where my bones shall be thrown: *corpse

A thousand thousand sighs to save,
  Lay me, O! where
Sad true lover never find my grave,
  To weep there!

Twelfth Night, Act 2, Scene 4

O Mistress Mine!

O mistress mine, where are you roaming?
O, stay and hear; your true love's coming,
  That can sing both high and low:
Trip no further, pretty sweeting;
Journeys end in lovers meeting,
  Every wise man's son doth know.

What is love? 'tis not hereafter;
Present mirth hath present laughter;
  What's to come is still unsure:
In delay there lies no plenty;
Then come kiss me, sweet and twenty,
  Youth's a stuff will not endure.

Twelfth Night, Act 2, Scene 3

Full Fathom Five

Full fathom five thy father lies;
  Of his bones are coral made;
Those are pearls that were his eyes:
  Nothing of him that doth fade
But doth suffer a sea-change
Into something rich and strange.
Sea-nymphs hourly ring his knell:
    Ding-dong
Hark! now I hear them—
  Ding-dong, bell.

The Tempest, Act 1, Scene 2

The Witches' Chant

A Cavern: in the middle, a boiling cauldron.
Thunder. Enter the three Witches

1st Witch	Thrice the brinded* cat hath mew'd.	*her familiar — a brindled, or striped cat
2nd Witch	Thrice and once the hedge-pig whined.	
3rd Witch	Harpier* cries 'Tis time, 'tis time.	*her familiar — a harpy
1st Witch	Round about the cauldron go;	
	In the poison'd entrails throw.	
	Toad, that under cold stone	
	Days and nights has thirty-one	
	Swelter'd* venom sleeping got,	*exuded like sweat
	Boil thou first i' the charmed pot.	
All	Double, double toil and trouble;	
	Fire burn, and cauldron bubble.	
2nd Witch	Fillet of a fenny snake,*	*a slice of snake from the fens
	In the cauldron boil and bake;	
	Eye of newt and toe of frog,	
	Wool of bat and tongue of dog,	
	Adder's fork and blind-worm's sting,	
	Lizard's leg and owlet's wing,	
	For a charm of powerful trouble,	
	Like a hell-broth boil and bubble.	
All	Double, double toil and trouble;	
	Fire burn and cauldron bubble.	
3rd Witch	Scale of dragon, tooth of wolf,	
	Witches' mummy,* maw and gulf	*dried flesh of human bodies
	Of the ravin'd* salt-sea shark,	*stomach of a glutted shark
	Root of hemlock* digg'd i' the dark...	*believed poisonous
	Add thereto a tiger's chaudron,	
	For the ingredients of our cauldron.	
All	Double, double toil and trouble;	
	Fire burn and cauldron bubble.	
2nd Witch	Cool it with a baboon's blood,	
	Then the charm is firm and good.	

Macbeth, Act 4, Scene 1

202

Sonnets

12

When I do count the clock that tells the time,
And see the brave day sunk in hideous night;
When I behold the violet past prime, *   *past its best
And sable* curls, all silvered o'er with white;   *black
When lofty trees I see barren of leaves,
Which erst* from heat did canopy* the herd,   *formerly *shelter
And summer's green all girded* up in sheaves,   *tied
Borne on the bier* with white and bristly beard,   *wagon, especially for
Then of thy beauty do I question make,   corpses
That thou among the wastes of time must go,
Since sweets and beauties do themselves forsake*   *cease to be so
And die as fast as they see others grow;
   And nothing 'gainst Time's scythe can make defence
   Save breed,* to brave him* when he takes thee hence.   *children *to defy him

106

When in the chronicle of wasted time*   *old stories of times past
I see descriptions of the fairest wights*,   *beautiful people; persons
And beauty making beautiful old rhyme,
In praise of ladies dead and lovely* knights,   *handsome
Then, in the blazon* of sweet beauty's best,   *list of good qualities
Of hand, of foot, of lip, of eye, of brow,
I see their antique pen would have express'd
Even such a beauty as you master* now.   *possess
So all their praises are but prophecies
Of this our time, all you prefiguring*;   *all offering prophetic images of you
And for* they looked but with divining* eyes,   *because *prophetic
They had not skill enough your worth to sing:
   For we, which now behold these present days,
   Have eyes to wonder, but lack tongues to praise.

116

Let me not* to the marriage of true minds
Admit impediments*. Love is not love
Which alters when it alteration finds,
Or bends with the remover to remove*:
O, no, it is an ever-fixed mark*,
That looks on tempests and is never shaken;
It is the star* to every wandering bark*,
Whose worth's unknown, although his height be taken*.
Love's not Time's fool*, though rosy lips and cheeks
Within his bending sickle's compass* come;
Love alters not with his* brief hours and weeks,
But bears it out* even to the edge of doom. *
    If this be error and upon me proved,
    I never writ, nor no man ever loved.

*May I never
*allow objections or obstacles
*changes when the loved
  person ceases to love
*unmoving landmark,
  e.g. lighthouse or star
*North star *ship
*position is measured
*plaything of Time
*curved sweep of the scythe
*i.e. Time's
*endures it *until doomsday

Unit 3
JOHN CLARE

John Clare
1793-1864. *'The peasant poet'*

John Clare, 'the peasant poet', was born in Northamptonshire, the son of a poor farm worker. John Clare had very little schooling. He was too poor to buy books and was thirteen before he scraped together enough money for two books of poetry. When he was very young he fell in love with Mary Joyce and he wrote poems about her all his life. In 1820 he married Patty Turner. In 1837 he was struck down with severe mental illness. He died in Northampton Asylum in 1864.

Clare loved the countryside and wrote beautifully about trees, flowers and the changing seasons. His best known collection of poems is *The Shepherd's Calendar* published in 1824.

The poems

I am

I am! yet what I am who cares, or knows?
    My friends forsake me like a memory lost.
I am the self-consumer of my woes;
    They rise and vanish, an oblivious host,
Shadows of life, whose very soul is lost.
And yet I am — I live — though I am toss'd

Into the nothingness of scorn and noise,
    Into the living sea of waking dream,
Where there is neither sense of life, nor joys,
    But the huge shipwreck of my own esteem
And all that's dear. Even those I loved the best
Are strange — nay, they are stranger than the rest.

I long for scenes where man has never trod —
    For scenes where women never smiled or wept —
There to abide with my Creator, God,
    And sleep as I in childhood sweetly slept,
Full of high thoughts, unborn. So let me lie, —
The grass below; above, the vaulted sky.

The Vixen

Among the taller wood with ivy hung,
The old fox plays and dances round her young.
She snuffs and barks if any passes by
And swings her tail and turns prepared to fly.
The horseman hurries by, she bolts to see,
And turns agen, from danger never free.
If any stands she runs among the poles
And barks and snaps and drives them in the holes.
The shepherd sees them and the boy goes by
And gets a stick and progs the hole to try.
They get all still and lie in safety sure,
And out again when everything's secure,
And start and snap at blackbirds bouncing by
To fight and catch the great white butterfly.

Pleasant Sounds

The rustling of leaves under the feet in woods and under
    hedges;
The crumping of cat-ice and snow down wood-rides, narrow
    lanes and every street causeway;
Rustling through a wood or rather rushing, while the wind
    halloos in the oak-top like thunder;
The rustle of birds' wings startled from their nests or flying
    unseen into the bushes;
The whizzing of larger birds overhead in a wood, such as
    crows, paddocks*, buzzards;   *kites
The trample of robins and woodlarks on the brown leaves,
    and the patter of squirrels on the green moss;
The fall of an acorn on the ground, the pattering of nuts on
    the hazel branches as they fall from ripeness;
The flirt of ground-lark's wing from the stubbles — how
    sweet such pictures on dewy mornings, when the dew
    flashes from its brown feathers!

Love

    Love lives beyond
The tomb, the earth, which fades like dew —
    I love the fond,
The faithful, and the true.

    Love lies in sleep,
The happiness of healthy dreams,
    Eve's dews may weep,
But love delightful seems.

    'Tis seen in flowers,
And in the even's pearly dew,
    On earth's green hours,
And in the heaven's eternal blue.

    'Tis heard in spring
When light and sunbeams, warm and kind,
    On angel's wing
Brings love and music to the wind.

And where is voice
So young and beautifully sweet
　　As nature's choice,
When spring and lovers meet?

　　Love lives beyond
The tomb, the earth, the flowers, and dew.
　　I love the fond,
The faithful, young, and true.

To Mary: it is the Evening Hour

It is the evening hour,
　　How silent all doth lie,
The hornèd moon he shews his face
　　In the river with the sky.
Just by the path on which we pass
The flaggy lake lies still as glass.

Spirit of her I love,
　　Whispering to me,
Stories of sweet visions, as I rove,
　　Here stop, and crop with me
Sweet flowers that in the still hour grew,
We'll take them home, nor shake off the bright dew.

Mary, or sweet spirit of thee,
　　As the bright sun shines to-morrow,
Thy dark eyes these flowers shall see,
　　Gathered by me in sorrow,
In the still hour when my mind was free
To walk alone — yet wish I walk'd with thee.

An Invite to Eternity

Wilt thou go with me, sweet maid,
Say, maiden, wilt thou go with me
Through the valley-depths of shade,
Of night and dark obscurity;
Where the path hath lost its way,
Where the sun forgets the day,
Where there's nor life nor light to see,
Sweet maiden, wilt thou go with me?

208

Where stones will turn to flooding streams,
Where plains will rise like ocean waves,
Where life will fade like visioned dreams
And mountains darken into caves,
Say, maiden, wilt thou go with me
Through this sad non-identity,
Where parents live and are forgot,
And sisters live and know us not?

Say, maiden; wilt thou go with me
In this strange death of life to be,
To live in death and be the same,
Without this life, or home, or name,
At once to be and not to be -
That was and is not – yet to see
Things pass like shadows, and the sky
Above, below, around us lie.

The land of shadows will thou trace
And look – nor know each other's face,
The present mixed with reasons gone
And past, and present all as one,
Say, maiden, can thy life be led
To join the living with the dead?
Then trace thy footsteps on with me,
We're wed to one eternity.

Unit 4

ALFRED, LORD TENNYSON

Alfred, Lord Tennyson
1809-1892

Alfred Tennyson was born in 1809, the fourth of twelve children. He started to write when he was a teenager and, at Cambridge, was encouraged in his writing by a close group of friends called 'The Apostles'. One of those friends, Arthur Hallam, died tragically young and Tennyson wrote one of his most famous poems *In Memoriam* published in his memory in 1850.

In the same year, Tennyson became poet laureate in succession to Wordsworth and in 1884 he became a peer. During the last 40 years of his life he was the most popular and famous poet of the period, seeming to represent the Victorian age in his appearance as well as his poetry. He was a large man with a powerful physique, usually made more impressive by a cloak and broad-brimmed hat, and a booming voice when he read his poems that captivated his audiences.

The poems

The selection here includes poems about birds and monsters which show different moods – from the threatening horror of *The Kraken*, to the impressive superiority of *The Eagle* and the light-hearted picture of *Song – The Owl*. These poems, together with *The Splendour Falls* also show Tennyson's skill in making the sounds of his words and the rhythms of the lines fit the subjects he is writing about.

There is also a ballad and one of the best-known narrative poems in the language, *The Lady of Shalott*. Tennyson's poems are known for their musical qualities, strong visual images and interesting stories – but he was also a thoughtful writer. The tiny poem *Flower in the Crannied Wall*, and his own 'poetic goodbye' to the world in *Crossing the Bar* find him questioning the meaning of life and death.

The Eagle

He clasps the crag with hookéd hands;
Close to the sun in lonely lands,
Ringed with the azure world, he stands.

The wrinkled sea beneath him crawls;
He watches from his mountain walls,
And like a thunderbolt he falls.

The Kraken *

*a mythical sea beast of gigantic size

Below the thunders of the upper deep,
Far, far beneath in the abysmal sea,
His ancient, dreamless, uninvaded sleep
The Kraken sleepeth: faintest sunlights flee
About his shadowy sides; above him swell
Huge sponges of millennial growth and height;
And far away into the sickly light,
From many a wondrous grot and secret cell
Unnumbered and enormous polypi *   *octopuses
Winnow with giant arms the slumbering green.
There hath he lain for ages, and will lie
Battening upon huge sea worms in his sleep,
Until the latter fire * shall heat the deep;   *fire that will finally consume the world
Then once by man and angels to be seen,
In roaring he shall rise and on the surface die.

Flower in the Crannied Wall

Flower in the crannied wall,
I pluck you out of the crannies,
I hold you here, root and all, in my hand,
Little flower – but if I could understand
What you are, root and all, and all in all,
I should know what God and man is.

From: The Princess

Sweet and low, sweet and low,
    Wind of the western sea,
Low, low, breathe and blow,
    Wind of the western sea!
Over the rolling waters go,
Come from the dying moon, and blow,
    Blow him again to me;
While my little one, while my pretty one,
    sleeps.

Sleep and rest, sleep and rest,
    Father will come to thee soon;
Rest, rest, on mother's breast,
    Father will come to thee soon;
    Father will come to his babe in the nest,
Silver sails all out of the west
    Under the silver moon:
Sleep, my little one, sleep, my pretty one,
    sleep.

Song – The Owl

I
When cats run home and light is come,
    And dew is cold upon the ground,
And the far-off stream is dumb,
    And the whirring sail goes round,
    And the whirring sail goes round;
      Alone and warming his five wits,
      The white owl in the belfry sits.

The Splendour Falls

The splendour falls on castle walls
    And snowy summits old in story:
The long light shakes across the lakes,
    And the wild cataract leaps in glory.
Blow, bugle, blow, set the wild echoes
    flying,
Blow, bugle; answer, echoes, dying, dying,
    dying.

O hark, O hear! how thin and clear,
    And thinner, clearer, farther going!
O sweet and far from cliff and scar
    The horns of Elfland faintly blowing!
Blow, let us hear the purple glens replying:
Blow, bugle; answer, echoes, dying, dying,
    dying.

O love, they die in yon rich sky,
    They faint on hill or field or river:
Our echoes roll from soul to soul,
    And grow for ever and for ever.
Blow, bugle, blow, set the wild echoes
    flying,
And answer, echoes, answer, dying, dying,
    dying.

II
When merry milkmaids click the latch,
    And rarely smells the new-mown hay,
And the cock hath sung beneath the thatch
    Twice or thrice his roundelay,
    Twice or thrice his roundelay;
      Alone and warming his five wits,
      The white owl in the belfry sits.

The Lady of Shalott

Part I

On either side the river lie
Long fields of barley and of rye,
That clothe the wold and meet the sky;
And thro' the field the road runs by
    To many-tower'd Camelot;
And up and down the people go,
Gazing where the lilies blow
Round an island there below,
    The island of Shalott.

Willows whiten, aspens quiver,
Little breezes dusk and shiver
Thro' the wave that runs for ever
By the island in the river
    Flowing down to Camelot.

Four gray walls, and four gray towers,
Overlook a space of flowers,
And the silent isle imbowers
    The Lady of Shalott.

By the margin, willow-veil'd,
Slide the heavy barges trail'd
By slow horses; and unhail'd
The shallop flitteth silken-sail'd
    Skimming down to Camelot:
But who hath seen her wave her hand?
Or at the casement seen her stand?
Or is she known in all the land,
    The Lady of Shalott?

Only reapers, reaping early
In among the bearded barley,
Hear a song that echoes cheerly
From the river winding clearly,
    Down to tower'd Camelot:
And by the moon the reaper weary,
Lifting sheaves in uplands airy,
Listening, whispers ''Tis the fairy
    Lady of Shalott.'

Part II

There she weaves by night and day
A magic web with colours gay.
She has heard a whisper say,
A curse is on her if she stay
    To look down to Camelot.
She knows not what the curse may be,
And so she weaveth steadily,
And little other care hath she,
    The Lady of Shalott.

And moving thro' a mirror clear
That hangs before her all the year,
Shadows of the world appear.
There she sees the highway near
    Winding down to Camelot:
There the river eddy whirls,
And there the surly village-churls,
And the red cloaks of market girls,
    Pass onward from Shalott.

Sometimes a troop of damsels glad,
An abbot on an ambling pad,
Sometimes a curly shepherd-lad,
Or long-hair'd page in crimson clad,
    Goes by to tower'd Camelot;
And sometimes thro' the mirror blue
The knights come riding two and two:
She hath no loyal knight and true,
    The Lady of Shalott.

But in her web she still delights
To weave the mirror's magic sights,
For often thro' the silent nights
A funeral, with plumes and lights
    And music, went to Camelot:
Or when the moon was overhead,
Came two young lovers lately wed;
'I am half sick of shadows,' said
    The Lady of Shalott.

Part III

A bow-shot from her bower-eaves,
He rode between the barley-sheaves,
The sun came dazzling thro' the leaves,
And flamed upon the brazen greaves
    Of bold Sir Lancelot.
A red-cross knight for ever kneel'd
To a lady in his shield,
That sparkled on the yellow field,
    Beside remote Shalott.

The gemmy bridle glitter'd free,
Like to some branch of stars we see
Hung in the golden Galaxy.
The bridle bells rang merrily
    As he rode down to Camelot:
And from his blazon'd baldric slung
A mighty silver bugle hung,
And as he rode his armour rung,
    Beside remote Shalott.

All in the blue unclouded weather
Thick-jewell'd shone the saddle-leather,
The helmet and the helmet-feather
Burn'd like one burning flame together,
    As he rode down to Camelot.
As often thro' the purple night,
Below the starry clusters bright,
Some bearded meteor, trailing light,
    Moves over still Shalott.

His broad clear brow in sunlight glow'd;
On burnish'd hooves his war-horse trode;
From underneath his helmet flow'd
His coal-black curls as on he rode,
    As he rode down to Camelot.
From the bank and from the river
He flash'd into the crystal mirror,
'Tirra lirra,' by the river
    Sang Sir Lancelot.

She left the web, she left the loom,
She made three paces thro' the room,
She saw the water-lily bloom,
She saw the helmet and the plume,
    She look'd down to Camelot.
Out flew the web and floated wide;
The mirror crack'd from side to side;
'The curse is come upon me,' cried
    The Lady of Shalott.

Part IV

In the stormy east-wind straining,
The pale yellow woods were waning,
The broad stream in his banks complaining,
Heavily the low sky raining
    Over tower'd Camelot;
Down she came and found a boat
Beneath a willow left afloat,
And round about the prow she wrote
    The Lady of Shalott.

And down the river's dim expanse
Like some bold seer in a trance,
Seeing all his own mischance –
With a glassy countenance
    Did she look to Camelot.
And at the closing of the day
She loosed the chain, and down she lay;
The broad stream bore her far away,
    The Lady of Shalott.

Lying, robed in snowy white
That loosely flew to left and right –
The leaves upon her falling light –
Thro' the noises of the night
    She floated down to Camelot:
And as the boat-head wound along
The willowy hills and fields among,
They heard her singing her last song,
    The Lady of Shalott.

Heard a carol, mournful, holy,
Chanted loudly, chanted lowly,
Till her blood was frozen slowly,
And her eyes were darken'd wholly,
    Turn'd to tower'd Camelot.
For ere she reach'd upon the tide
The first house by the water-side,
Singing in her song she died,
    The Lady of Shalott.

Under tower and balcony,
By garden-wall and gallery,
A gleaming shape she floated by,
Dead-pale between the houses high,
    Silent into Camelot.
Out upon the wharfs they came,
Knight and burgher, lord and dame,
And round the prow they read her name
    The Lady of Shalott.

Who is this? and what is here?
And in the lighted palace near
Died the sound of royal cheer:
And they cross'd themselves for fear,
    All the knights at Camelot;
But Lancelot mused a little space;
He said, 'She has a lovely face;
God in his mercy lend her grace,
    The Lady of Shalott.'

Crossing the Bar *

Sunset and evening star,
    And one clear call for me!
And may there be no moaning of the bar *,
    When I put out to sea.

But such a tide as moving seems asleep,
    Too full for sound and foam,
When that which drew from out the boundless deep
    Turns again home.

Twilight and evening bell,
    And after that the dark!
And may there be no sadness of farewell,
    When I embark;

For though from out our bourne * of Time and Place
    The flood may bear me far,
I hope to see my Pilot face to face
    When I have crossed the bar.

*this poem was chosen by Tennyson to be the last in his collection

*mournful sound of the sea on a sand bar at the harbour mouth

*boundary

Unit 5
CHRISTINA ROSSETTI

Christina Rossetti
1830-1894

Christina Rossetti was born into an Anglo-Italian family which had strong religious convictions and a great love of the arts. These two influences are reflected in her life and her writing. She lived quietly, caring for her family, working for charity and writing poems. Twice she planned to marry but, on both occasions, her religious principles led her to call off the engagement.

Christina Rossetti's brother was Dante Gabriel Rossetti, part of a famous group of painters called The Pre-Raphaelite Brotherhood. Like the Pre-Raphaelite painters, Rossetti often took nature as her subject and tried to depict it in precise detail, as in the poem *Spring* (page **219**). She wrote in a range of different styles and this collection includes sonnets, lyric verse, narrative fable and even a Christmas carol. These poems show an awareness of the role of women, a belief in the afterlife and, perhaps most revealing of all, the idea of preserving a secret space for oneself (*Winter: My Secret* page **223**).

The poems

In an Artist's Studio

One face looks out from all his canvases,
    One selfsame figure sits or walks or leans:
    We found her hidden just behind those screens,
That mirror gave back all her loveliness.
A queen in opal or in ruby dress,
    A nameless girl in freshest summer-greens,
    A saint, an angel – every canvas means
The same one meaning, neither more nor less.
He feeds upon her face by day and night,
    And she with true kind eyes looks back on him,
Fair as the moon and joyful as the light:
    Not wan with waiting, not with sorrow dim;
Not as she is, but was when hope shone bright;
    Not as she is, but as she fills his dream.

Up-Hill

Does the road wind up-hill all the way?
  Yes, to the very end.
Will the day's journey take the whole long day?
  From morn to night, my friend.

But is there for the night a resting-place?
  A roof for when the slow dark hours begin.
May not the darkness hide it from my face?
  You cannot miss that inn.

Shall I meet other wayfarers at night?
  Those who have gone before.
Then must I knock, or call when just in sight?
  They will not keep you standing at that door.

Shall I find comfort, travel-sore and weak?
  Of labour you shall find the sum.
Will there be beds for me and all who seek?
  Yea, beds for all who come.

Song

When I am dead, my dearest,
  Sing no sad songs for me;
Plant thou no roses at my head,
  Nor shady cypress tree:
Be the green grass above me
  With showers and dewdrops wet;
And if thou wilt, remember,
  And if thou wilt, forget.

I shall not see the shadows,
  I shall not feel the rain;
I shall not hear the nightingale
  Sing on, as if in pain;
And dreaming through the twilight
  That doth not rise nor set,
Haply I may remember,
    And haply may forget.

Spring

Frost-locked all the winter,
Seeds, and roots, and stones of fruits,
What shall make their sap ascend
That they may put forth shoots?
Tips of tender green,
Leaf, or blade or sheath;
Telling of the hidden life
That breaks forth underneath,
Life nursed in its grave by Death.

Blows the thaw-wind pleasantly,
Drips the soaking rain,
By fits looks down the waking sun:
Young grass springs on the plain;
Young leaves clothe early hedgerow trees;
Seeds, and roots, and stones of fruits,
Swollen with sap put forth their shoots;
Curled-headed ferns sprout in the lane;
Birds sing and pair again.

There is no time like Spring,
When life's alive in everything,
Before new nestlings sing,
Before cleft swallows speed their journey back
Along the trackless track—
God guides their wing,
He spreads their table that they nothing lack,—
Before the daisy grows a common flower,
Before the sun has power
To scorch the world up in his noontide hour.

There is no time like Spring,
Like Spring that passes by:
There is no life like Spring-life born to die,—
Piercing the sod,
Clothing the uncouth clod,
Hatched in the nest,
Fledged on the windy bough,
Strong on the wing;
There is no time like Spring that passes by,
Now newly born, and now
Hastening to die.

A Christmas Carol

In the bleak mid-winter
  Frosty wind made moan,
Earth stood hard as iron,
  Water like a stone;
Snow had fallen snow on snow,
  Snow on snow,
In the bleak mid-winter
  Long ago.

Our God, Heaven cannot hold Him
  Nor earth sustain;
Heaven and earth shall flee away
  When He comes to reign;
In the bleak mid-winter
  A stable-place sufficed
The Lord God Almighty
  Jesus Christ.

Enough for Him, whom cherubim
  Worship night and day,
A breastful of milk
  And a mangerful of hay;
Enough for Him, whom angels
  Fall down before,
The ox and ass and camel
  Which adore.

Angels and archangels
  May have gathered there,
Cherubim and seraphim
  Thronged the air;
But only His mother
  In her maiden bliss
Worshipped the Beloved
  With a kiss.

What can I give Him?
  Poor as I am?
If I were a shepherd
  I would bring a lamb,
If I were a Wise Man
  I would do my part,—
Yet what can I give him,
  Give my heart.

Remember

Sonnet

Remember me when I am gone away,
  Gone far away into the silent land;
  When you can no more hold me by the hand,
Nor I half turn to go, yet turning stay.
Remember me when no more day by day
  You tell me of our future that you plann'd:
  Only remember me; you understand
It will be late to counsel then or pray.
Yet if you should forget me for a while
  And afterwards remember, do not grieve:
  For if the darkness and corruption leave
  A vestige of the thoughts that once I had,
Better by far you should forget and smile
Than that you should remember and be sad.

The Caterpillar

Brown and furry
Caterpillar in a hurry,
Take your walk
To the shady leaf, or stalk,
  Or what not,
Which may be the chosen spot.
  No toad spy you,
Hovering bird of prey pass by you;
Spin and die,
To live again as a butterfly.

Winter: My Secret

I tell my secret? No indeed, not I:
Perhaps some day, who knows?
But not today; it froze, and blows, and snows,
And you're too curious: fie!
You want to hear it? well:
Only, my secret's mine, and I won't tell.

Or, after all, perhaps there's none:
Suppose there is no secret after all,
But only just my fun.
Today's a nipping day, a biting day;
In which one wants a shawl,
A veil, a cloak, and other wraps:
I cannot ope to every one who taps,
And let the draughts come whistling thro' my hall;
Come bounding and surrounding me,
Come buffeting, astounding me,
Nipping and clipping thro' my wraps and all.
I wear my mask for warmth: who ever shows
His nose to Russian snows
To be pecked at by every wind that blows?
You would not peck? I thank you for good will,
Believe, but leave that truth untested still.

Spring's an expansive time: yet I don't trust
March with its peck of dust,
Nor April with its rainbow-crowned brief showers,
Nor even May, whose flowers
One frost may wither thro' the sunless hours.

Perhaps some languid summer day,
When drowsy birds sing less and less,
And golden fruit is ripening to excess,
If there's not too much sun nor too much cloud,
And the warm wind is neither still nor loud,
Perhaps my secret I may say,
Or you may guess.

D.H.LAWRENCE

D.H. Lawrence
1885 – 1930

D.H Lawrence (his full name was David Herbert Lawrence) is better known as a writer of novels but he was also a considerable poet.

Lawrence was brought up in a pit village where his father was a coal miner. However his mother was determined that Lawrence should not work in the mine and, after doing well at school, he eventually became a teacher and, later, a writer. He married Frieda Weekly in 1912.

Lawrence wrote passionately about human relationships, particularly those of ordinary people, about politics and class divisions and about the natural world. He could be fierce about those things he despised but he could be tender about the things he loved. *Last Lesson of the Afternoon* (page **225**) recalls his not altogether happy career as a teacher; the tender dialect poem *Violets* (page **229**) shows his eye (and ear) for a small village drama; and a poem like *Wages* (page **228**), shows his fury at the way workers were both exploited and allowed themselves to be exploited.

The poems

Last Lesson of the Afternoon

When will the bell ring, and end this weariness?
How long have they tugged the leash, and strained apart,
My pack of unruly hounds! I cannot start
Them again on a quarry of knowledge they hate to hunt,
I can haul them and urge them no more.

No longer now can I endure the brunt
Of the books that lie out on the desks; a full threescore
Of several insults of blotted pages, and scrawl
Of slovenly work that they have offered me.
I am sick, and what on earth is the good of it all?
What good to them or me, I cannot see!

        So, shall I take
My last dear fuel of life to heap on my soul
And kindle my will to a flame that shall consume
Their dross of indifference; and take the toll
Of their insults in punishment? — I will not! —

I will not waste my soul and my strength for this.
What do I care for all that they do amiss!
What is the point of this teaching of mine, and of this
Learning of theirs? It all goes down the same abyss.

What does it matter to me, if they can write
A description of a dog, or if they can't?
What is the point? To us both, it is all my aunt!
And yet I'm supposed to care, with all my might.

I do not, and will not; they won't and they don't;
 and that's all!
I shall keep my strength for myself; they can keep
 theirs as well.
Why should we beat our heads against the wall
Of each other? I shall sit and wait for the bell.

Kangaroo

In the northern hemisphere
Life seems to leap at the air, or skim under the wind
Like stags on a rocky ground, or pawing horses, or springy
      scut-tailed rabbits.

Or else rush horizontal to charge at the sky's horizon,
Like bulls or bisons or wild pigs.

Or slip like water slippery towards its ends,
As foxes, stoats, and wolves, and prairie dogs.

Only mice, and moles, and rats, and badgers, and beavers, and
      perhaps bears
Seem belly-plumbed to the earth's mid-navel.
Or frogs that when they leap come flop, and flop to the centre of
      the earth.

But the yellow antipodal Kangaroo, when she sits up,
Who can unseat her, like a liquid drop that is heavy and just
      touches earth.

The downward drip
The down-urge.
So much denser than cold-blooded frogs.

Delicate mother Kangaroo
Sitting up there rabbit-wise, but huge, plumb-weighted,
And lifting her beautiful slender face, Oh! so much more gently
      and finely lined than a rabbit's, or than a hare's,
Lifting her face to nibble at a round white peppermint drop
      which she loves, sensitive mother Kangaroo.

Her sensitive, long, pure-bred face.
Her full antipodal eyes, so dark,
So big and quiet and remote, having watched so many empty
      dawns in silent Australia.

Her little loose hands, and drooping Victorian shoulders.
And then her great weight below the waist, her vast pale belly
With a thin young yellow little paw hanging out, and a straggle of
      a long thin ear, like ribbon.
Like a funny trimming to the middle of her belly, thin little
      dangle of an immature paw, and one thin ear.

Her belly, her big haunches
And, in addition, the great muscular python-stretch of her tail.

There, she shan't have any more peppermint drops.
So she wistfully, sensitively sniffs the air, and then turns, goes
        off in slow sad leaps.

On the long flat skis of her legs,
Steered and propelled by that steel-strong snake of a tail.

Stops again, half turns, inquistive to look back.
While something stirs quickly in her belly, and a lean little face
        comes out, as from a window,

Peaked and a bit dismayed,
Only to disappear again quickly away from the sight of the
        world, to snuggle down in the warmth
Leaving the trail of a different paw hanging out.

Still she watches with eternal, cocked wistfulness!
How full her eyes are, like the full, fathomless, shining eyes of
        an Australian black-boy
Who has been lost so many centuries on the margins of
        existence!

She watches with insatiable wistfulness.
Untold centuries of watching for something to come,
For a new signal from life, in that silent lost land of the South.

Where nothing bites but insects and snakes and the sun, small
        life.
Where no bull roared, no cow ever lowed, no stag cried, no
        leopard screeched, no lion coughed, no dog barked,
But all was silent save for parrots occasionally, in the haunted
        blue bush.
Wistfully watching, with wonderful liquid eyes.
And all her weight, all her blood, dripping sack-wise down
        towards the earth's centre,
And the live little-one taking in its paw at the door of her belly.

Leap then, and come down the line that draws to the earth's
        deep, heavy centre.

Baby Running Barefoot

When the white feet of the baby beat across the grass
The little white feet nod like white flowers in a wind,
They poise and run like puffs of wind that pass
Over water where the weeds are thinned.

And the sight of their white playing in the grass
Is winsome as a robin's song, so fluttering:
Or like two butterflies that settle on a glass
Cup for a moment, soft little wing-beats uttering.

And I wish that the baby would tack across here to me
Like a wind-shadow running on a pond, so she could stand
With two little bare white feet upon my knee
And I could feel her feet in either hand

Cool as syringa buds in morning hours,
Or firm and silken as young peony flowers.

Wages

The wages of work is cash.
The wages of cash is want more cash.
The wages of want more cash is vicious competition.
The wages of vicious competition is – the world we live in.

The work-cash-want circle is the viciousest circle
that ever turned men into fiends.

Earning a wage is a prison occupation
and a wage-earner is a sort of gaol-bird.
Earning a salary is a prison overseer's job,
a gaoler instead of a gaol-bird.

Living on your income is strolling grandly outside the prison
in terror lest you have to go in. And since the work-prison covers
almost every scrap of the living earth, you stroll up and down
on a narrow beat, about the same as a prisoner taking his exercise.

This is called universal freedom.

New Houses, New Clothes

New houses, new furniture, new streets, new clothes, new sheets
everything new and machine-made sucks life out of us
and makes us cold, makes us lifeless
the more we have.

Things Men Have Made

Things men have made with wakened hands, and put soft
 life into
are awake through years with transferred touch, and go
 on glowing
for long years.
And for this reason, some old things are lovely
warm still with the life of forgotten men who made them.

Violets

Sister, tha knows* while we was on th' planks   *you know
 Aside o' t' grave, an' th' coffin set
On th' yaller* clay, wi' th' white flowers top of it   *yellow
 Waitin' ter be buried out o' th' wet?

An' t' parson makin' haste, an' a' t' black
 Huddlin' up i' t' rain,
Did t' 'appen ter notice a bit of a lass way back
 Hoverin', lookin' poor an' plain?

 — How should I be lookin' round!
  An' me standin' there on th' plank,
  An' our Ted's coffin set on th' ground,
  Waitin' to be sank!

 I'd as much as I could do, to think
  Of 'im bein' gone
 That young, an' a' the fault of drink
  An' carryin's on! —

Let that be; 'appen it worna* th' drink, neither,   *was not
Nor th' carryin' on as killed 'im.
                        —No, 'appen not,
My sirs!* But I say 'twas! For a blither†   *exclamation of angry contempt
Lad never stepped, till 'e got in with your lot. —   † happier

All right, all right, it's my fault! But let
Me tell about that lass. When you'd all gone
Ah stopped behind on t' pad, i' t' pourin' wet
An' watched what 'er 'ad on.

Tha should ha' seed 'er slive up* when yer'd gone!   *sidle up
Tha should ha' seed 'er kneel an' look in
At th' sloppy grave! an' 'er little neck shone
That white, an' 'er cried that much, I'd like to begin

Scraightin'* mysen as well. 'Er undid 'er black   *crying
Jacket at th' bosom, an' took out
Over a double 'andful o' violets, a' in a pack   *tangle
An' white an' blue in a ravel*, like a clout†.   † bunch of frayed cloth

An' warm, for th' smell come waftin' to me. 'Er put 'er face
Right in 'em, an' scraighted a bit again,
Then after a bit 'er dropped 'em down that place,
An' I come away, acause o' th' teemin' rain.

But I thowt* ter mysen, as that wor th' only bit   *thought
O' warmth as 'e got down theer; th' rest wor stone cold.
From that bit of a wench's bosom; 'e'd be glad of it,
Gladder nor of thy lilies, if tha maun* be told.   *must

Unit 7

TED HUGHES

Ted Hughes

1930 – 1998

Ted Hughes was born in Yorkshire, the son of a carpenter. He excelled at school and won a scholarship to the University of Cambridge. He had many different jobs including a gardener, zookeeper and teacher. In 1956 he married the American poet Sylvia Plath. They had two children but the marriage was often unhappy and Sylvia Plath committed suicide in 1963.

Ted Hughes is best known for his powerful poems about animals and the natural world. His first collection of poems 'The Hawk in the Rain' was published in 1957. Other volumes followed in steady succession. Some of them were for the general reader but others, for example, 'Season Songs' and 'Under the North Star', were written for children. The huge success, particularly of his poems about animals, led to his being created Poet Laureate in 1984.

The poems

Hughes' poems are never cosy or sentimental poems. They often celebrate the raw and elemental energy of nature. In *To Paint a Water Lily*, he points to the contrast between the seeming beauty of the lily above the surface 'whatever horror nudge her root'. In *October Dawn* a glass of wine left outside overnight is found with a skim of ice on its surface next morning which to Hughes suggests the return of the ice age. His view of nature can be both bleak and harsh, reflecting the battle for survival which underlies all of nature.

October Dawn

October is marigold, and yet
A glass half full of wine left out

To the dark heaven all night, by dawn
Has dreamed a premonition

Of ice across its eye as if
The ice-age had begun its heave.

The lawn overtrodden and strewn
From the night before, and the whistling green

Shrubbery are doomed. Ice
Has got its spearhead into place.

First a skin, delicately here
Restraining a ripple from the air;

Soon plate and rivet upon pond and brook;
Then tons of chain and massive lock

To hold rivers. Then, sound by sight
Will Mammoth and Sabre-tooth celebrate

Reunion while a fist of cold
Squeezes the fire at the core of the world,

Squeezes the fire at the core of the heart,
And now it is about to start.

To Paint a Water Lily

A green level of lily leaves
Roofs the pond's chamber and paves

The flies' furious arena: study
These, the two minds of this lady.

First observe the air's dragonfly
That eats meat, that bullets by

Or stands in space to take aim;
Others as dangerous comb the hum

Under the trees. There are battle-shouts
And death-cries everywhere hereabouts

But inaudible, so the eyes praise
To see the colours of these flies

Rainbow their arcs, spark, or settle
Cooling like beads of molten metal

Through the spectrum. Think what worse
Is the pond-bed's matter of course;

Prehistoric bedragonned times
Crawl that darkness with Latin names,

Have evolved no improvements there,
Jaws for heads, the set stare,

Ignorant of age as of hour—
Now paint the long-necked lily-flower

Which, deep in both worlds, can be still
As a painting, trembling hardly at all

Though the dragonfly alight,
Whatever horror nudge her root.

The Warm and the Cold

Freezing dusk is closing
  Like a slow trap of steel
On trees and roads and hills and all
  That can no longer feel.
    But the carp is in its depth
      Like a planet in its heaven.
    And the badger in its bedding
      Like a loaf in the oven.
    And the butterfly in its mummy
      Like a viol in its case.
    And the owl in its feathers
      Like a doll in its lace.

Freezing dusk has tightened
  Like a nut screwed tight
On the starry aeroplane
  Of the soaring night.
    But the trout is in its hole
      Like a chuckle in a sleeper.
    The hare strays down the highway
      Like a root going deeper.
    The snail is dry in the outhouse
      Like a seed in a sunflower.
    The owl is pale on the gatepost
      Like a clock on its tower.

Moonlight freezes the shaggy world
  Like a mammoth of ice—
The past and the future
  Are the jaws of a steel vice.
    But the cod is in the tide-rip
      Like a key in a purse.
    The deer are on the bare-blown hill
      Like smiles on a nurse.
    The flies are behind the plaster
      Like the lost score of a jig.
    Sparrows are in the ivy-clump
      Like money in a pig.

Such a frost
  The flimsy moon
    Has lost her wits.

        A star falls.

The sweating farmers
  Turn in their sleep
    Like oxen on spits.

Snowdrop

Now is the globe shrunk tight
Round the mouse's dulled wintering heart.
Weasel and crow, as if moulded in brass,
Move through an outer darkness
Not in their right minds,
With the other deaths. She, too, pursues her ends,
Brutal as the stars of this month,
Her pale head heavy as metal.

Gulls

Gulls are glanced from the lift
Of cliffing air
And left
Loitering in the descending drift,
Or tilt gradient and go
Down steep invisible clefts in the grain
Of air, blading against the blow,

Back-flip, wisp
Over the foam-galled green
Building seas, and they scissor
Tossed spray, shave sheen,
Wing-waltzing their shadows
Over the green hollows,

Or rise again in the wind's landward rush
And, hurdling the thundering bush
With the stone wall flung in their faces,
Repeat their graces.

Full Moon and Little Frieda

A cool small evening shrunk to a dog bark and the clank
 of a bucket –

And you listening.
A spider's web, tense for the dew's touch.
A pail lifted, still and brimming – mirror
To tempt a first star to a tremor.

Cows are going home in the lane there, looping the
     hedges with their warm wreaths of breath –
A dark river of blood, many boulders,
Balancing unspilled milk.

'Moon!' you cry suddenly, 'Moon! Moon!'

The moon has stepped back like an artist gazing amazed
     at a work

That points at him amazed.

Mooses

The goofy Moose, the walking house-frame,
Is lost
In the forest. He bumps, he blunders, he stands.

With massy bony thoughts sticking out near his ears—
Reaching out palm upwards, to catch whatever might be
    falling from heaven—
He tries to think,
Leaning their huge weight
On the lectern of his front legs.

He can't find the world!
Where did it go? What does a world look like?
The Moose
Crashes on, and crashes into a lake, and stares at the
    mountain, and cries
'Where do I belong? This is no place!'

He turns and drags half the lake out after him
And charges the cackling underbrush—

He meets another Moose.
He stares, he thinks 'It's only a mirror!'

'Where is the world?' he groans, 'O my lost world!
And why am I so ugly?
And why am I so far away from my feet?'

He weeps.
Hopeless drops drip from his droopy lips.

The other Moose just stands there doing the same.

Two dopes of the deep woods.

Unit 8

JOHN AGARD

John Agard
1949 –

John Agard was born in British Guiana (now Guyana). He came to England in 1977 and worked for the Commonwealth Institute giving readings, talks and workshops on Caribbean culture and poetry. He was the first Poet in Residence at the BBC and has published many volumes of poetry. His partner is the poet Grace Nichols.

John Agard's poems often seem light-hearted but they also make some serious points, as in *Half-caste* (page 240) and *Stereotype* (page 241). His poems are written to be spoken and performed, not just read. They are full of rhythm, influenced by the music and speech of the Caribbean.

The poems

The three books drawn upon most for this selection are *Mangoes and Bullets* (Serpent's Tail, 1985), *Get Back Pimple* (Puffin, 1997) and *We Brits* (Bloodaxe, 2006). We begin with a group of light-hearted poems written with young people in mind. Three poems, *Half-caste*, *Stereotype*, and *From Britannia To Whom It May Concern*, draw the reader in with the same humour and then, by the end, make the reader think about the serious point behind the words. As you may have seen in his poem *Rainbow* (page **63**), John Agard's poems often produce a 'thoughtful smile' when we read them. *Newton's Amazing Grace*, a poem about a slave ship captain who converted to the ministry and wrote a famous hymn, concludes the selection.

Poetry Jump-Up

Tell me if Ah seeing right
Take a look down de street

Words dancin
words dancin
till dey sweat
words like fishes
jumpin out a net
words wild and free
joinin de poetry revelry
words back to back
words belly to belly

Come on everybody
come and join de poetry band
dis is poetry carnival
dis is poetry bacchanal
when inspiration call
take yu pen in yu hand
if yu don't have a pen
take yu pencil in yu hand
if yu don't have a pencil
what the hell
so long de feeling start to swell
just shout de poem out

Words jumpin off de page
tell me if Ah seein right
words like birds
jumping out a cage
take a look down de street
words shakin dey waist
words shakin dey bum
words wit black skin
words wit white skin
words wit brown skin
words wit no skin at all
words huggin up words
an sayin I want to be a poem today
rhyme or no rhyme
I is a poem today
I mean to have a good time

Words feeling hot hot hot
big words feeling hot hot hot
lil words feeling hot hot hot
even sad words cant help
tappin dey toe
to de riddum of de poetry band

Dis is poetry carnival
dis is poetry bacchanal
so come on everybody
join de celebration
all yu need is plenty perspiration
an a little inspiration
plenty perspiration
an a little inspiration

Not-Enough-Pocket-Money Blues

I could see myself stepping light and slow
in them jeans
so hip-sharp-tight and full-of-flow.
Could just ...
But I've got me the no-cash no-dosh
not-enough-pocket-money blues.

Could see myself slinking to school
in them trainers
so jaguar-sleek and puma-cool.
Could just ...
But I've got me the no-cash no-dosh
not-enough-pocket-money blues.

Could see myself a fashion queen
in that top
so flirty-smart and snazzy-sleeved.
Could just ...
But I've got me the no-cash no-dosh
not-enough-pocket-money blues.

Could see myself all summery
in that hat
so patchwork-wicked and flowery.
Could just ...
But I've got me the no-cash no-dosh
not-enough-pocket-money blues.

I guess I can always ask Mum.

239

Spell to Banish a Pimple

Get back pimple
get back to where you belong

Get back to never-never land
and I hope you stay there long

Get back pimple
get back to where you belong

How dare you take residence
in the middle of my face

I never offered you a place
beside my dimple

Get back pimple
get back to where you belong

Get packing pimple
I banish you to outer space

If only life was that simple

A Date with Spring

Got a date with Spring
Got to look me best.
Of all the trees
I'll be the smartest dressed.

Perfumed breeze
behind me ear.
Pollen accessories
all in place.
Raindrop moisturizer
for me face.
Sunlight tints
to spruce up the hair.

What's the good of being a tree
if you can't flaunt your beauty?

Winter, I was naked.
Exposed as can be.
Me wardrobe took off
with the wind.
Life was a frosty slumber
Now, Spring, here I come
Can't wait to slip in
to me little green number.

Child Waiting
(for Lesley)

little head
at the window
in childeyed wonder

the ceaseless
come and go
of mighty traffic
must be moving magic
to your unblinking gaze

but how patient
are eyes looking for one
named mummy
in a rumble of wheels

Half-caste

Excuse me
standing on one leg
I'm half-caste

Explain yuself
wha yu mean
when yu say half-caste
yu mean when picasso
mix red an green
is a half-caste canvas/
explain yuself
wha yu mean
when yu say half-caste
yu mean when light an shadow
mix in de sky
is a half-caste weather/
well in dat case
england weather
nearly always half-caste
in fact some o dem cloud
half-caste till dem overcast
so spiteful dem dont want de sun pass
ah rass/
explain yuself
wha yu mean
when yu say half-caste
yu mean when tchaikovsky
sit down at dah piano
an mix a black key
wid a white key
is a half-caste symphony/

240

Explain yuself
wha yu mean
Ah listening to yu wid de keen
half of mih ear
Ah lookin at yu wid de keen
half of mih eye
an when I'm introduced to you
I'm sure you'll understand
why I offer yu half-a-hand
an when I sleep at night
I close half-a-eye
consequently when I dream
I dream half-a-dream
an when moon begin to glow
I half-caste human being
cast half-a-shadow
but yu must come back tomorrow

wid de whole of yu eye
an de whole of yu ear
an de whole of yu mind

an I will tell yu
de other half
of my story

Stereotype

I'm a fullblooded
West Indian stereotype
See me straw hat?
Watch it good

I'm a fullblooded
West Indian stereotype
You ask
if I got riddum
in me blood
You going ask!
Man just beat de drum
and don't forget
to pour de rum

I'm a fullblooded
West Indian stereotype
You say
I suppose you can show
us the limbo, can't you?
How you know!
How you know!
You sure
you don't want me
sing you a calypso too
How about that

I'm a fullblooded
West Indian stereotype
You call me
happy-go-lucky
Yes that's me
dressing fancy
and chasing woman
if you think ah lie
bring yuh sister

I'm a fullblooded
West Indian stereotype
You wonder
where do you people
get such riddum
could it be the sunshine
My goodness
just listen to that steelband

Isn't there one thing
you forgot to ask
go on man ask ask
This native will answer anything
How about cricket?
I suppose you're good at it?
Hear this man
good at it!
Put de willow
in me hand
and watch me stripe
de boundary

241

Yes I'm a fullblooded
West Indian stereotype

that's why I
graduated from Oxford University
with a degree
in anthropology

From Britannia To Whom It May Concern

Thank you for the kind thought, the compliment
of even calling me mother country.
You make an island feel like a continent.

When I ruled the waves, all the world seemed pink.
I manipulated maps with sword and cross.
Shifted boundaries with seal of royal ink.

I enthroned my language as a rule of tongue,
Gathered India's jewels into my crown.
And Africa's blood still haunts my monuments.

How can I turn from history's looking-glass
when even my sugar holds a bitter past?
The sea has been my girdle and my guilt.

Though darkness enriches my red white and blue,
I've learnt how the sun sets on empires,
And the voiceless voice their righteous fires.

Now, old ruptures bless me with hybrid webs.
I feel horizons throbbing at my doorstep.
My streets pulse with a plurality of tongues.

And mother country has much work to do.
I must prepare my cliffs for new homecomings.
Tie yellow ribbons round my children's minds.

Newton's Amazing Grace

(John Newton (1725–1807), slave ship captain, who converted to the ministry and composed many hymns including 'Amazing Grace'.)

Grace is not a word for which I had much use.
And I skippered ships that did more than bruise
the face of the Atlantic. I carved my name
in human cargo without a thought of shame.
But the sea's big enough for a man to lose
his conscience, if not his puny neck.
In the sea's eye, who is this upstart speck
that calls himself a maker of history?
It took a storm to save the dumb wretch in me.
On a night the winds weighed heavy as my sins,
I spared a thought for those poor souls below deck.
Terror made rough waters my Damascus road.
Amazing grace began to lead me home.
Lord, let my soul's scum be measured by a hymn.

CHARLES CAUSLEY

Charles Causley
1917–2003

Charles Causley was born in Launceston, Cornwall. In the Second World War he joined the navy and, after the war, became a teacher. He continued to teach and write for the rest of his life. Charles Causley was fascinated by the sea and by the myths and legends of his native Cornwall. There is often a sense of mystery, magic and sometimes even terror lurking behind his poems which, like *Mary, Mary Magdalene* (page **245**) and *The Ballad of Charlotte Dymond* (page **121**) are often written in ballad form.

Charles Causley wrote many different types of poems including war poetry, religious poetry and poems for children. He also liked to write about paintings, especially those with religious themes, as in *Coming from Evening Church* (page **247**).

The poems

Mary, Mary Magdalene

On the east wall of the Church of St Mary Magdalene at Launceston in Cornwall is a granite figure of the saint. The children of the town say that a stone lodged on her back will bring good luck.

Mary, Mary Magdalene
Lying on the wall,
I throw a pebble on your back.
Will it lie or fall?

Send me down for Christmas
Some stockings and some hose,
And send before the winter's end
A brand new suit of clothes.

Mary, Mary Magdalene
Under a stony tree,
I throw a pebble on your back.
What will you send me?

*I'll send you for your christening
A woollen robe to wear,
A shiny cup from which to sup,
And a name to bear.*

Mary, Mary Magdalene
Lying cool as snow,
What will you be sending me
When to school I go?

*I'll send a pencil and a pen
That write both clean and neat,
And I'll send to the schoolmaster
A tongue that's kind and sweet.*

Mary, Mary Magdalene
Lying in the sun,
What will you be sending me
Now I'm twenty-one?

*I'll send you down a locket
As silver as your skin
And I'll send you a lover
To fit a gold key in.*

Mary, Mary Magdalene
Underneath the spray,
What will you be sending me
On my wedding-day?

*I'll send you down some blossom,
Some ribbons and some lace,
And for the bride a veil to hide
The blushes on her face.*

Mary, Mary Magdalene
Whiter than the swan,
Tell me what you'll send me,
Now my good man's dead and gone.

*I'll send to you a single bed
On which you must lie,
And pillows bright where tears may light
That fall from your eye.*

Mary, Mary Magdalene
Now nine months are done.
What will you be sending me
For my little son?

*I'll send you for your baby
A lucky stone, and small
To throw to Mary Magdalene
Lying on the wall.*

245

I Saw a Jolly Hunter

I saw a jolly hunter,
    With a jolly gun
Walking in the country
    In the jolly sun.

In the jolly meadow
    Sat a jolly hare.
Saw the jolly hunter
    Took jolly care.

Hunter jolly eager –
    Sight of jolly prey.
Forgot gun pointing
    Wrong jolly way.

Jolly hunter jolly head
    Over heels gone.
Jolly old safety catch
    Not jolly on.

Bang went the jolly gun
    Hunter jolly dead.
Jolly hare got clean away
    Jolly good I said.

My Mother Saw A Dancing Bear

My mother saw a dancing bear
By the schoolyard, a day in June.
The keeper stood with chain and bar
And whistle-pipe, and played a tune.

And bruin lifted up its head
And lifted up its dusty feet,
And all the children laughed to see
It caper in the summer heat.

They watched as for the Queen it died.
They watched it march. They watched it
    halt.
They heard the beggar as he cried,
'Now, roly-poly!' 'Somersault!'

And then, my mother said, there came
The keeper with a begging-cup,
The bear with burning coat of fur,
Shaming the laughter to a stop.

They paid a penny for the dance,
But what they saw was not the show;
Only in bruin's aching eyes,
Far distant forests, and the snow.

Eden Rock

They are waiting for me somewhere beyond
    Eden Rock:
My father, twenty-five, in the same suit
Of Genuine Irish Tweed, his terrier Jack
Still two years old and trembling at his feet.

My mother, twenty-three, in a sprigged
    dress
Drawn at the waist, ribbon in her straw hat,
Has spread the stiff white cloth over the
    grass.
Her hair, the colour of wheat, takes on the
    light.

She pours tea from a Thermos, the milk
    straight
From an old H.P. sauce-bottle, a screw
Of paper for a cork; slowly sets out
The same three plates, the tin cups painted
    blue.

The sky whitens as if lit by three suns.
My mother shades her eyes and looks my way
Over the drifted stream. My father spins
A stone along the water. Leisurely,

They beckon to me from the other bank.
I hear them call, 'See where the stream-
    path is!
Crossing is not as hard as you might think.'
I had not thought that it would be like this.

Samuel Palmer's Coming from Evening Church

The heaven-reflecting, usual moon
Scarred by thin branches, flows between
The simple sky, its light half-gone,
The evening hills of risen green.
Safely below the mountain crest
A little clench of sheep holds fast.
The lean spire hovers like a mast
Over its hulk of leaves and moss
And those who, locked within a dream,
Make between church and cot their way
Beside the secret-springing stream
That turns towards an unknown sea;
And there is neither night or day,
Sorrow nor pain eternally.

GRACE NICHOLS

Grace Nichols
1950 –

Grace Nichols was born in Guyana where she attended university and later became a journalist. She came to England in 1977 and has become a well-known author and poet. Her first book of poetry *i is a long memoried woman* won the Commonwealth poetry prize. Her partner is the poet John Agard.

Grace Nichols often writes about historical themes – from her own childhood to the story of the Afro-Caribbean people. Some poems, like *Praise Song for my Mother* (page **250**), contain warm memories of her Caribbean childhood, others, like *Taint* (page **252**), reflect more distant memories of slavery and oppression. Grace Nichols often uses Creole words in her poems and is strongly influenced by Caribbean language and rhythms.

The poems

Epilogue

I have crossed an ocean
I have lost my tongue
From the root of the old one
A new one has sprung.

Baby-K rap rhyme

My name is Baby-K

An dis is my rhyme

Sit back folks

While I rap my mind;

Ah rocking with my homegirl,

My Mommy

Ah rocking with my homeboy,

My Daddy

My big sister, Les, an

My Granny,

Hey dere people – my posse

I'm the business

The ruler of the nursery

poop po-doop

poop-poop po-doop

poop po-doop

poop-poop po-doop

Well, ah soaking up de rhythm

Ah drinking up my tea

Ah bouncing an ah rocking

On my Mommy knee

So happy man so happy

poop po-doop

poop-poop po-doop

poop po-doop

poop-poop po-doop

Wish my rhyme wasn't hard

Wish my rhyme wasn't rough

But sometimes, people

You got to be tough

Cause dey pumping up de chickens

Dey stumping down de trees

Dey messing up de ozones

Dey messing up de seas

Baby-K say, stop dis –

please, please, please

poop po-doop

poop-poop po-doop

poop po-doop

poop-poop po-doop

Now am splashing in de bath

With my rubber duck

Who don't like dis rhyme

Kiss my baby-foot

Babies everywhere

Join a Babyhood

Cause dey hotting up de globe, man

Dey hitting down de seals

Dey killing off de ellies

for dere ivories

Baby-K say, stop dis –

please, please, please

poop po-doop

poop-poop po-doop

poop po-doop

poop-poop po-doop

Dis is my Baby-K rap

But it's kinda plea

What kinda world

Dey going to leave fuh me?

What kinda world

Dey going to leave fuh me?

Poop po-doop.

Praise Song for My Mother

You were
water to me
deep and bold and fathoming

you were
moon's eye to me
pull and grained and mantling

You were
sunrise to me
rise and warm and streaming

You were
the fishes red gill to me
the flame tree's spread to me
the crab's leg/the fried plantain smell
replenishing replenishing

Go to your wide futures, you said.

Wherever I Hang

I leave me people, me land, me home
For reasons I not too sure
I forsake de sun
And de humming-bird splendour
Had big rats in de floorboard
So I pick up me new-world-self
And come to this place call England
At first I feeling like I in a dream –
De misty greyness
I touching the walls to see if they real
They solid to de seam
And de people pouring from de underground system
Like beans
And when I look up to de sky
I see Lord Nelson high – too high to lie.
And is so I sending home photos of myself
Among de pigeons and de snow
And is so I warding off de cold
And is so, little by little
I begin to change my calypso ways
Never visiting nobody
Before giving them clear warning
And waiting me turn in queue
Now, after all this time
I get accustom to de English life
But I still miss back-home side
To tell you de truth
I don't know really where I belaang

      Yes, divided to de ocean
      Divided to de bone

Wherever I hang me knickers – that's my home.

Taint

But I was stolen by men
the colour of my own skin
borne away by men whose heels
had become hoofs
whose hands had turned talons
bearing me down
        to the trail
of darkness

But I was traded by men
the colour of my own skin
traded like a fowl   like a goat
like a sack of kernels I was
traded
        for beads   for pans
for trinkets?

No it isn't easy to forget
what we refuse to remember

Daily I rinse the taint
of treachery from my mouth.

We the Women

We the women who toil
unadorn
heads tie with cheap
cotton

We the women who cut
clear fetch dig sing

We the women making
something from this
ache-and-pain-a-me
back-o-hardness

Yet we the women
who praises go unsung
who voices go unheard
who deaths they sweep
aside
as easy as dead leaves

Looking at Miss World

Tonight the fat black woman
is all gaze
will some Miss (plump at least
if not fat and black) uphold her name

The fat black woman awaits in vain
slim after aspirant appears
baring her treasures in hopeful despair
this the fat black woman can hardly bear

And as the beauties yearn
and the beauties yearn
the fat black woman wonders
when will the beauties
ever really burn

O the night wears on
the night wears on
judges mingling with chiffons

The fat black woman gets up
and pours some gin
toasting herself as a likely win

252

Waterpot

The daily going out
and coming in
always being hurried
along
like like... cattle

In the evenings
returning from the fields
she tried hard to walk
like a woman

she tried very hard
pulling herself erect
with every three or four
steps
pulling herself together
holding herself like
royal crane*   *African bird

And the overseer
hurrying them along
in the quickening darkness

And the overseer sneering
them along on in the quickening
darkness
sneered at the pathetic
the pathetic display
of dignity

O but look
there's a waterpot growing
from her head

Snowflake

Little shaving
of hot white cold
Snowflake
Snowflake
you really bold

How you feeling, Snowflake?
Icily-Hot
How you feeling, Snowflake?
Ice-Silly-Hot

Snowflake
Snowflake
you little clown

```
          c
           a
            r
          n
        i
      v
      a
      l
        l
          i
           n
            g
            d
              o
            w
          n
```
A small ghost kiss
on my warm tongue.

Skanking* Englishman Between Trains   *walking in reggae rhythm

Met him at Birmingham Station
small yellow hair Englishman
hi fi stereo swinging in one hand
walking in rhythm to reggae sound/Man

he was alive
he was full-o-jive
said he had a lovely
Jamaican wife

Said he couldn't remember
the taste of English food
I like mih drops
me Johnny cakes
me peas and rice
me soup/Man

he was alive
he was full-o-jive
said he had a lovely
Jamaican wife

Said, showing me her photo
whenever we have a little quarrel
you know/to sweeten her up
I surprise her with a nice mango/Man

he was alive
he was fill-o-jive
said he had a lovely Jamaican wife

GLOSSARY

Alliteration	Repeated consonant sounds, e.g. "flattening my fur…" from *Cat*, page 10
Assonance	Repeated vowel sounds, e.g. "the hush and touch of the sudden warm air" from *Cat*, page 10
Ballad	Poem that tells a story, usually written in four line verses, often including a repeated chorus or **refrain**
Blank verse	Unrhymed verse with a basic five-beat rhythm
Calligram	Poem where the words trace the outline of their subject, e.g. *Amazed Cat*, page 6
Choral	Several voices speaking
Cliché	Over-used comparison, e.g. "As light as a feather."
Concrete poem	Poem where letters or words are arranged to reflect the poem's subject or meaning, e.g. *Revolver*, page 4
Couplet	A pair of rhyming lines, usually of the same length. For example, the lines in *Motherless Baby*, page 44
Dialect	Particular language used in different parts of the country
Duet	Performance by two people
Elegy	Poem remembering someone who has died
Free verse	Poetry with no regular **metre** or **rhyme** pattern
Haiku	Type of poem, originating in Japan, consisting of 17 syllables, arranged in lines of five, seven and five syllables. English versions are often less rigid in structure. See pages 14 – 16
Image	Picture or impression conveyed in words by a writer
Limerick	Five-line poem (usually humorous) where the longer lines (1, 2 and 5) rhyme with each other as do the shorter lines (3 and 4). See pages 3 and 4
List poems	Poem listing objects or emotions, usually following a repetitive pattern
Metaphor	Direct comparison of one thing with another without using "as" or "like". For example, "He is the knight at arms breaking the fields' Mirror of Silence…" from *Cynddylan on a Tractor*, page 19
Metre	The rhythmic arrangement of syllables in a poem

255

Glossary

Onomatopoeia	Words that sound like the thing described, e.g. the words "glubbery slobbery gloopery" to describe cleaning a sticky porridge pan on page 41
Personification	Giving a human character to something non-human, e.g. Edmund Spenser's poem on page 64 making the sin of gluttony into a loathsome person
Refrain	Chorus or repeated line
Rhyme	Words that end with exactly the same sound, e.g. "right" and "fight"
Rhyme scheme	Pattern of rhyming in a poem. Often, when describing a poem, we give each line a letter so that we can say whether line A rhymes with line B or line C. Rhyming lines are given the same letter. For example, the rhyme scheme of *Sir Patrick Spens* on pages 57 – 59 is ABCB
Rhythm	The pattern of sound in a poem, its beat, e.g. the insistent rhythm of *The Quarry*, page 32
Silhouette poem	Poem arranged in the solid shape of its subject, e.g. *Guitar*, page 3
Simile	Comparison using "as" or "like", e.g. "As red as a rose", page 20
Solo	Performance by one person
Sonnet	Poem in a strict form. A sonnet always consists of 14 lines, sometimes arranged as 8 lines (the octave) followed by six lines (the sextet) and sometimes as three sets of four lines (quatrains) plus a **couplet**
Stress	The emphasis placed on a word, e.g. in the word "Monday", the first syllable is stressed, the second unstressed
Syllable	Sounds that make up words. For example, the word 'underneath' has three syllables: un-der-neath
Symbol	Something that represents something else. For example, a dove is a symbol of peace
Tongue Twister	Poem or phrase that is deliberately hard to say
Trio	Three people performing
Triplet	Three lines that rhyme with each other

ACKNOWLEDGEMENTS

The editors and publisher wish to thank the following for permission to reproduce copyright material:

ANNA ADAMS: 'Warning To A Worm' from *A Paper Ark* (Peterloo Poets, 1999), reproduced by permission of the publisher; **JOHN AGARD**: 'Woodpecker' copyright © 1991 by John Agard, 'Rainbow' copyright © 1983 by John Agard, 'Snowflake' copyright © 1997 by John Agard and 'Child waiting' copyright © 1985 by John Agard from *Mangoes and Bullets* (Serpent's Tail, 1997); 'Poetry Jump-Up', 'Not Enough Pocket Money Blues', 'A Date with Spring', 'Half-Caste', 'From Britannia', 'Newton's Amazing Grace' and 'Spell to Banish a Pimple' from *Get Back, Pimple!* (Puffin, 1997), copyright © 1996 by John Agard; 'Stereotype' copyright © 1983 by John Agard from *We Brits* (Bloodaxe, 2006), reproduced by kind permission of John Agard c/o Caroline Sheldon Literary Agency Limited; **MONIZA ALVI**: 'I Would Like to be a Dot in a Painting by Miró' from *Split World: Poems:1990-2005* (Bloodaxe Books, 2008), reproduced by permission of the publisher; **MAYA ANGELOU**: 'Sepia Fashion Show' from *Just Give Me a Cool Drink of Water 'Fore I Diiie* (Virago, 1988); 'Life Doesn't Frighten Me' from *And Still I Rise* (Virago, 1986),reproduced by permission of Little, Brown Book Group; **GUILLAUME APOLLINAIRE**: 'The Evening Star', translated by Oliver Bernard, from *Selected Poems* (Penguin Modern European Poets, 1965), translation copyright © Oliver Bernard, 1965; **SIMON ARMITAGE**: 'Learning by Rote' from *Tyrannosaurus Rex Versus the Corduroy Kid* (Faber & Faber, 2007); **W. H. AUDEN**: 'The Quarry' and 'Musée des Beaux Arts' from *Collected Shorter Poems, 1927 - 1957* (Faber & Faber, 1969); **GITA BEDI**: ''Ere She Said' from *Grass Roots in Verse* (Hansib, 1988), reproduced by permission of the publisher; **PETER BENTON**: 'James' copyright © Peter Benton; **MORRIS BISHOP**: 'Song of the Pop Bottlers' from *The New Yorker*, copyright © 1950; **KEITH BOSLEY**: 'How to Address a Goldfish' from *And I Dance* (Angus & Robertson (UK), 1972), copyright © Keith Bosley, reproduced by permission of the author; **KAMAU BRATHWAITE**: 'Limbo' from *The Arrivants* (Oxford University Press, 1981), reproduced by permission of the publisher; **KWESI BREW**: 'The Mash' and 'The Dry Season' from *Shadows of Laughter* (Longman, 1968); **ALAN BROWNJOHN**: 'Cat' from *The Book of Cats,* edited by George Macbeth and Martin Booth (Penguin Books, 1979); **CHARLES CAUSLEY**: 'Infant Song, What has Happened to Lulu', 'Tell Me, Tell Me Sarah Jane', 'Miller's End', 'The Ballad of Charlotte Dymond','Mary, Mary Magdalene', 'I Saw a Jolly Hunter', 'My Mother Saw a Dancing Bear', 'Eden Rock', 'A Village in Heaven' and 'Samuel Palmer's Coming from Evening Church' from *Collected Poems* (Picador, 2000), reproduced by permission of David Higham Associates; **DEBJANI CHATTERJEE**: 'My Sari' from *Unzip Your Lips: 100 Poems to Read Aloud*, chosen by Paul Cookson (Macmillan, 1998), reproduced by permission of the author; **KATE CLANCHY**: 'Timetable' from *Slattern* (Chatto and Windus, 1996), reproduced by permission of Pan Macmillan, London; **GILLIAN CLARKE**: 'Legend' from *Five Fields* (Carcanet Press, 1998), reproduced by permission of the publisher; **MARGARET POSTGATE COLE**: 'The Veteran' from *An Anthology of War Poems*, edited by Frederick Brereton (William Collins, 1930), reproduced by permission of David Higham Associates; **TONY CONNOR**: 'A Child Half-Asleep' from *Kon in Springtime* (Oxford University Press, 1968), **WENDY COPE**: 'Tich Miller' from *Making Cocoa for Kingsley Amis* (Faber & Faber, 1986), copyright Wendy Cope 1986, reproduced by permission of PFD (www.pfd.co.uk) on behalf of Wendy Cope; **FRANCES CORNFORD**: 'Childhood' from *Collected Poems* (The Cresset Press, 1954), reproduced by kind permission of the Trustees of the Mrs F.C. Cornford Deceased Will Trust; **KEVIN CROSSLEY-HOLLAND**: 'My Breast is Puffed Up' from *Storm and Other Old English Riddles* (Macmillan, 1970), copyright © Kevin Crossley-Holland, reproduced by permission of the author c/o Rogers, Coleridge & White Ltd., 20 Powis Mews, London W11 1JN; **E. E. CUMMINGS**: 'in Just-' and 'hist whist' from *Complete Poems, 1904–1962* (Liveright, 1994), copyright © 1991 by the Trustees for the E.E. Cummings Trust and George James Firmage, reproduced by permission of W.W. Norton & Company; **PAUL DEHN**: 'Alternative Endings To an Unwritten Ballad' and 'Exercise Book' from *Fern on the Rock, Collected Poems 1935/65* (Hamish Hamilton, 1965), reproduced by permission of Berlin Associates; **WALTER DE LA MARE**: 'Echo', 'The Listeners' and 'The Ghost' from *Collected Poems* (Faber & Faber, 1979), reproduced by permission of The Literary Trustees of Walter de la mare and the Society of Authors as their representative; **EMILY DICKINSON**: 'The spider holds a silver ball' from *The Poems of Emily Dickinson*, Thomas H. Johnson, ed., Cambridge, Mass.: The Belknap Press of Harvard University Press, copyright © 1951, 1955, 1979, 1983 by the President and Fellows of Harvard Colege, reproduced by permission of the publishers and the Trustees of Amherst College; **KEVIN DICKSON**: 'Amazed cat' copyright © Kevin Dickson; **CAROL ANN DUFFY**: 'In Mrs Tilsher's Class' from *The Other Country* (Anvil Press Poetry, 1990); 'Time Transfixed by *Rene Magritte*' copyright © Carol Ann Duffy; **MARRIOT EDGAR**: 'The Lion and Albert' from *The Lion and Albert* (Methuen Publishing, 1978); **EFSTATHIOS**: 'The Ballad of Bovver Pete' copyright © Efstathios; **T. S. ELIOT**: 'Macavity: The Mystery Cat' from *Old Possum's Book of Practical Cats* (Faber & Faber, 1974); **ELAINE FEINSTEIN**: 'At Seven A Son' from *In a Green Eye* (Goliard Press, 1966); **ROBERT FROST**: 'Stopping by Woods on a Snowy Evening' and 'The Runaway' from *The Poetry of Robert Frost*, edited by Edward Connery Lathem (Jonathan Cape, 1971), reproduced by permission of The Random House Group Ltd; **WILFRID GIBSON**: 'Flannan Isle' from *Collected Poems, 1905–1925* (Macmillan, 1926), reproduced by permission of Pan Macmillan, London; **EDWARD GOREY**: 'Each Night Father Fills Me with Dread' from "The Listing Attic" in *Amphigorey: Fifteen Stories* (Perigee Books, 2004, by arrangement with The Edward Gorey Charitable Trust), reproduced by permission of The Edward Gorey Charitable Trust; **HARRY GRAHAM**: 'The Stern Parent' and 'Appreciation' from *Ruthless Rhymes for Heartless Homes* (Edward Arnold, 1974), copyright © The Trustees of Mrs V. M. Thesiger deceased, reproduced by permission of William Sturges & Co. (Solicitors); **SOPHIE HANNAH**: 'Summary of a Western' from *The Hero and the Girl Next Door* (Carcanet Press, 1995), reproduced by permission of the publisher; **HEATHER HARVEY**: 'Time Transfixed' copyright © Heather Harvey; **SEAMUS HEANEY**: 'Death of a Naturalist' from *Death of a Naturalist* (Faber & Faber, 2006); **JOHN HEATH-STUBBS**: 'The History of the Flood' from *Selected Poems* (Carcanet Press, 1990), reproduced by permission of David Higham Associates; **HAROLD G. HENDERSON**: 'Full moon', 'Summer Night', 'In the Moonlight', 'The Barleyfield', 'In the House' and 'Parting' from *An Introduction to Haiku* (Doubleday, 1958), copyright © 1958 by Harold G. Henderson, reproduced by permission of Doubleday, a division of Random House, Inc; **ADRIAN HENRI**: 'Love Is' from *The Mersey Sound* (Penguin Modern Classics, 2007), copyright © Estate of Adrian Henri, reproduced by permission of the author's estate c/o Rogers, Coleridge & White Ltd., 20 Powis Mews, London W11 1JN; **PHOEBE HESKETH**: 'Cats' and 'Sally' from *The Leave Train: New and Selected Poems* (Enitharmon Press, 1997), reproduced by permission of the publisher; **MIROSLAV HOLUB**: 'A Boy's Head' from *Selected Poems*, translated by Ian Milner and George Theiner, introduction by A. Alvarez (Penguin Books, 1967), copyright © Miroslav Holub,

1967, translation copyright © Penguin Books, 1967, reproduced by permission of the publisher; **TED HUGHES**: 'A Donkey', 'Wind', 'From Spring Nature Notes', 'Work and Play', 'Leaves' , 'October Dawn', 'To Paint a Water Lily', 'The Warm and the Cold', 'Snowdrop', 'Gulls', 'Full Moon and Little Frieda' and 'Moses' from *Collected Poems* (Faber & Faber, 2003); **ELIZABETH JENNINGS**: 'Hatching', 'Old People' and 'Spell of Air' from *A Spell of Words* (Macmillan Children's Books, 1997), reproduced by permission of David Higham Associates; **JENNY JOSEPH**: 'Warning' from *Selected Poems* (Bloodaxe Books, 1992), reproduced by kind permission of Johnson & Alcock Ltd; **JACKIE KAY**: 'Brendon Gallacher' and 'English Cousin Comes to Scotland' from *Two's Company* (Blackie, 1992), copyright © Jackie Kay, 1992, reproduced by permission of Penguin Books Ltd; 'Old Tongue' from *Darling: New & Selected Poems* (Bloodaxe Books, 2008), reproduced by permission of the publisher; **RICHARD KELL**: 'Pigeons' from *Differences* (Chatto & Windus, 1969), reproduced by permission of The Random House Group Ltd; **SUE KELLY**: 'Cat' copyright © Sue Kelly; **JAMES KIRKUP**: 'Baby's Drinking Song' from *White Shadows, Black Shadows* (Dent, 1970), reproduced by permission of the author; **PHILIP LARKIN**: 'First Sight' from *Collected Poems* (Faber & Faber, 1988), reproduced by permission of The Society of Authors as the Literary Representative of the Estate of Philip Larkin; 'Born Yesterday' from *Collected Poems* (Faber & Faber, 1988), copyright © the Estate of Philip Larkin, 1988; **J. A. LINDON**: from 'Sink Song' copyright © J. A. Lindon; **EDWARD LUCIE-SMITH**: 'The Lesson' from *A Tropical Childhood and Other Poems* (Oxford University Press, 1961), copyright © Edward Lucie-Smith, reproduced by permission of the author c/o Rogers, Coleridge & White Ltd., 20 Powis Mews, London W11 1JN; **ROGER MCGOUGH**: 'Oxygen' and 'The Railings' from *Defying Gravity* (Viking, 1992), copyright © Roger McGough 1992, reproduced by permission of PFD (www.pfd.co.uk) on behalf of Roger McGough; **DON MARQUIS**: 'The Tom-Cat' from *Poems & Portraits* (Doubleday, 1922); **SPIKE MILLIGAN**: 'Ye Tortures' from *A Dustbin of Milligan* (Dennis Dobson, 1961), reproduced by permission of Spike Milligan Productions Limited; **ADRIAN MITCHELL**: 'Back in the Playground Blues' copyright © Adrian Mitchell; **EDWIN MORGAN**: 'The Loch Ness Monster's Song' from *Collected Poems* (Carcanet Press, 1990), reproduced by permission of the publisher; **GRACE NICHOLLS**: 'Epilogue' from **The Fat Black Women's Poems** (Virago, 1984), reproduced by permission of Curtis Brown Group Ltd on behalf of the author.; **GRACE NICHOLS**: 'Baby-K Rap Rhyme', 'Praise Song for my Mother', 'Wherever I hang', 'Taint', 'We the Women', 'Looking at Miss World', 'Waterpot', 'Skanking Englishman' and 'Snowflake' from *Give Yourself a Hug* (A & C Black, 1994), copyright © Grace Nichols 1994; 'Epilogue' from *The Fat Black Woman's Poems* (Virago, 1984), copyright © Grace Nichols 1984, reproduced by permission of Curtis Brown Group Ltd; **NORMAN NICHOLSON**: 'The Imprint of a Seashell on a Stone' from *Collected Poems* (Faber & Faber, 1994), reproduced by permission of David Higham Associates; **JULIE O'CALLAGHAN**: 'Spring', 'Winter' Two Poems by Guiseppe Archimboldo from *Taking my Pen for a Walk* (Orchard, 1988), reproduced by permission of the author; **GARETH OWEN**: 'Boredom', 'Street Boy' and 'Icarus by Mobile' from *Salford Road* (Viking, 1979); **BRIAN PATTEN**: 'Little Johnny's Final Letter' and 'A Small Dragon' from *Selected Poems* (Penguin Books, 2007), copyright © Brian Patten, reproduced by permission of the author c/o Rogers, Coleridge & White Ltd., 20 Powis Mews, London W11 1JN; **STEF PIXNER**: 'Term Begins Again' from *Sawdust and White Spirit* (Virago, 1985), reproduced by permission of the author; **SYLVIA PLATH**: 'Morning Song' and 'Balloons' from *Collected Poems* (Faber & Faber, 1981); **EZRA POUND**: 'In a Station of a Metro' from *Selected Poems, 1908 - 1969* (Faber & Faber, 1977); **ALAN RIDDELL**: 'Guitar' and 'Revolver II' from *ECLIPSE, Concrete Poems 1963–1971* (Caldar and Boyars, 1972), copyright © The Estate of Alan Riddel and John Calder Publishers Ltd, 1972, reproduced by permission of Calder Publications (UK) Ltd; **ROBIN ROBERTSON**: 'La Stanza delle Mosche' from *Swithering* (Picador, 2006), reproduced by permission of Pan Macmillan, London; **MICHAEL ROSEN**: 'Going Through the Old Photos' and 'Lizzie' from *Quick Lets get Out of Here* (Puffin Books, 1985), reproduced by permission of Penguin Books Ltd; **COLIN ROWBOTHAN**: 'Rain Haiku' copyright © Colin Rowbotham; **CAROLE SATYAMURTI**: 'Leaving Present' from *Selected Poems* (Blodaxe Books, 200), reproduced by permission of the author; **W.C. SELLAR and R.J. YEATMAN**: 'How they brought…' (Methuen, 1930); **SENI SENEVIRATNE**: 'People Ask' from *Wish I Was Here: a Scottish multicultural anthology* (Pocketbooks, 2000); **HAMID SHAMI**: 'Lost' from *Wish I Was Here: a Scottish multicultural anthology* (Pocketbooks, 2000); **OWEN SHEERS**: 'Not Yet my Mother' from *The Blue Book* (Seren Books, 2000); **STEVIE SMITH**: 'This Englishwoman' from *The Collected Poems of Stevie Smith* (Allen Lane, 1975), copyright © Estate of James MacGibbon, reproduced by permission of James & James (Publishers) Ltd; **JON STALLWORTHY**: 'Sindhi Woman' from *Rounding the Horn, Collected Poems* (Carcanet Press, 1998), reproduced by permission of the publisher; **R.S. THOMAS**: 'Cynddylan on a Tractor', 'Children's Song' from *Collected Poems* (Phoenix, 2000); **HENRY TREECE**: 'The Magic Wood' from *Black Seasons* (Faber & Faber, 1945), copyright © the Estate of Henry Treece, reproduced by kind permission of Johnson & Alcock Ltd; **SARAH WARDLE**: 'Household Haiku' from *Fields Away* (Bloodaxe Books, 2002), reproduced by permission of the Publisher; **WILLIAM CARLOS WILLIAMS**: 'Landscape with the Fall of Icarus' from *Collected Poems 1939–62* (Carcanet Press, 1989), reproduced by permission of the publisher; **ANDREW YOUNG**: 'Hard Frost' and 'The Eagle' from *Selected Poems* (Carcanet Press,1998), reproduced by permission of the publisher; **BENJAMIN ZEPHANIAH**: 'Dis Poetry' from *City Psalms* (Bloodaxe Books, 1992), reproduced by permission of the publisher; 'Talking Turkeys' from *Talking Turkeys* (Viking, 1994), copyright © Benjamin Zephaniah, 1994); 'Serious Luv' from *Funky Chickens* (Viking, 1996), © Benjamin Zephaniah, 1996, reproduced by permission of Penguin Books Ltd.

Every effort has been made to establish copyright and contact copyright holders prior to publication. If contacted, the publisher will be pleased to rectify any omissions or errors at the earliest opportunity.